OECD Development Pathways

Multi-dimensional Review of Myanmar

VOLUME 3. FROM ANALYSIS TO ACTION

This work is published under the responsibility of the Secretary-General of the OECD. The opinions expressed and arguments employed herein do not necessarily reflect those of the OECD, its Development Centre or of their member countries.

This document and any map included herein are without prejudice to the status of or sovereignty over any territory, to the delimitation of international frontiers and boundaries and to the name of any territory, city or area.

Please cite this publication as:
OECD (2016), *Multi-dimensional Review of Myanmar: Volume 3. From Analysis to Action*, OECD Development Pathways, OECD Publishing, Paris.
http://dx.doi.org/10.1787/9789264256545-en

ISBN 978-92-64-25653-8 (print)
ISBN 978-92-64-25654-5 (PDF)
ISBN 978-92-64-25741-2 (ePub)

Series: OECD Development Pathways
ISSN 2308-734X (print)
ISSN 2308-7358 (online)

The statistical data for Israel are supplied by and under the responsibility of the relevant Israeli authorities. The use of such data by the OECD is without prejudice to the status of the Golan Heights, East Jerusalem and Israeli settlements in the West Bank under the terms of international law.

Photo credits: Cover design by the OECD Development Centre based on images © Kstudija, Kozoriz Yuriy, Seita, Robert Adrian Hillman, SoleilC, PILart/Shutterstock.com.

Corrigenda to OECD publications may be found on line at: *www.oecd.org/about/publishing/corrigenda.htm*.

Foreword

In 2013 the OECD launched the Multi-dimensional Country Reviews (MDCR), a new tool for tailoring broad OECD expertise to the realities of developing economies. Policy makers need to reconcile economic, social and environmental objectives to ensure that their country's development path is sustainable and that the lives of citizens improve. To support this need, the MDCRs aim to design policies and strategies which do not simply promote growth but rather development in this more comprehensive sense.

The Republic of the Union of Myanmar was the first country to engage in a Multi-dimensional Country Review and the OECD worked closely with stakeholders in the country throughout the review's three phases. In Phase 1, the review diagnosed the main constraints to development across a number of dimensions. This phase culminated with the publication of the Multi-dimensional Review of Myanmar Volume 1: Initial Assessment *that was launched in Myanmar in July 2013. Phase 2 focused on the critical areas for development identified in the first phase – structural transformation, education and skills, and financing development – by undertaking in-depth analysis to develop policy recommendations. The results of this phase were published in the* Multi-dimensional Review of Myanmar Volume 2: In-depth analysis and recommendations *that was launched in Myanmar in January 2015. In Phase 3, the recommendations were prioritised and further developed through stakeholder consultations in two policy dialogue events held in Myanmar in May and December 2015.*

This final report synthesises the full review process, summarising the findings from the diagnostic phase and the policy recommendations developed in the second phase, organised according to priority as defined by participants of the policy dialogue events.

Acknowledgements

The third phase of the Multi-dimensional Review of Myanmar was prepared by a team from the OECD Development Centre led by Jan Rieländer, Head of Multi-dimensional Country Reviews under the direction of Mario Pezzini, Director, OECD Development Centre: Martha Baxter, Deirdre Culley, Iris Chan and Richard Clarke. The team are grateful for the guidance and active participation of Rintaro Tamaki, OECD Deputy Secretary General. Administrative support was assured by Myriam Andrieux and Vararat Atisophon provided statistical assistance. The Development Centre's publication team, in particular Delphine Grandrieux and Elizabeth Nash turned the draft into a publication. The cover was designed by Aida Buendia.

The third phase would not have been possible without important collaborations:

U Tun Tun Naing, Permanent Secretary, Ministry of National Planning and Economic Development and his team at the Foreign and Economic Relations Department for their partnership in the Review process, participation in and logistical support for the events, comments on the report, as well as co-ordination with other ministries.

Raoul Blindenbacher, Senior Fellow at the Global Health Program of the Graduate Institute of International and Development Studies and founder of the Governmental Learning Lab worked with the team to design the policy dialogue events and was indispensable in his role as the knowledge broker.

Linda Fulponi, former OECD Senior Agricultural Economist and currently visiting professor at Yangon Institute of Economics, led the Review's work on agriculture and rural development and played an active role in the policy dialogue event and finalisation of this report.

The team from the Hanns Seidel Foundation Myanmar office for their organisation of the two policy dialogue events which took place on 29-30 May 2015 in Yangon and 10 December 2015 in Nay Pyi Taw: Achim Munz, Resident Representative; Michael Siegner, Programme Manager; Betty Phyu Lin, Trainee, and Aung Kyaw Phyo, Independent Consultant.

This report draws on the first two volumes of the Multi-dimensional Review of Myanmar, but also from the input from participants in the policy dialogue events:

U Tun Tun Naing, Permanent Secretary, Ministry of National Planning and Economic Development; U Than Aung Kyaw, Deputy Director General, Ministry of President's Office 5; U Myint Soe, Assistant Secretary, Ministry of Commerce; U Myint Wai, Director, Ministry of Commerce; Daw Win Min Phyoe Deputy Director, Ministry of Commerce; U Thaung Oo, Director, Ministry of Industry; Daw Moe Kyi Win, Deputy Director, Department of Agriculture, Ministry of Agriculture and Irrigation; Dr Kyaw Min Tun, Deputy Director, Department of Technological and Vocational Education, Ministry of Science and Technology; Dr Tin Moe Hlaing, Deputy Director, Biotechnology and Material Science Research Department, Ministry of Science and Technology; Dr Thinn Thinn Wah Assistant Director, Biotechnology and

Material Science Research Department, Ministry of Science and Technology; Khin Nan Myint, Deputy General Manager, MADB; Daw Yin Yin Aye, Director, Center for Vocational Training in Yangon; U Tin Htut Oo, Chairman, National Economic and Social Advisory Council; U Ziwa Naing, Director, National Economic and Social Advisory Council; U Min Khin, Member, Economic Committee, National League for Democracy; U Han Shwe, CEC, National Unity Party; U Thein Tun, CEC, National Unity Party; Dr Soe Tun, Joint Secretary General, Myanmar Rice Federation and Myanmar Farmers Association; U Soe Tun, Vice President, Myanmar Fisheries Federation; Dr Hla Hla Thein, Vice President, Meat and Livestock Federation, Managing Director Green Field International Co, Ltd; Dr Min Zaw, Vice Chairman, Vice President of Yangon Region Chamber of Commerce and Industry (Bayintnaung Commodity Exchange Center); U Soe Win Maung, Advisor to pulses, beans and sesame seeds Merchants' Associations; U Zar Ni Thwe, Agriculture and Farmers Federation of Myanmar (AFFM-IUF); Dr Nay Myo Aung, Lecturer, Agricultural Economics Department, Yezin Agricultural University; Dr Khin Mar Cho, International Agriculture, Food and Nutrition Specialist, Cornell University; U Kyaw Lin Oo, Executive Director, Myanmar People Forum Working Group; U Win Myo Thu, Managing Director, Ecodev; Dr Win May Htway, Country Manager, Path NGO; Ms Carin Salerno, Counsellor, Deputy Director of Co-operation, Embassy of Switzerland, Swiss Agency for Development and Co-operation; Ms. Khin Mya Mya Htwe, Deputy Director, Department of Trade, Ministry of Commerce; U Saw San Myint, AFFM-IUF; U Naing Thein Aung, Secretary for Organizing Department, AFFM-IUF; Professor Dr. San Win, Pro-rector, University of Forestry, Yezin; Dr. Joern Kristensen, Executive Director, Myanmar Institute for Integrated Development; Prof Dr Kyaw Kyaw Moe, University of Vet Sciences, Yezin; Dr Pinlone Aye, Assistant Director, FERD; Khin Ma Ma Bo, Staff Officer, FERD; Khin Maung Nyo, Chairman, Myanmar Economic Association; Khin Mya Mya Htway, Deputy Director, Ministry of Commerce; Kyaw Dun, Assistant Secretary, Ministry of Co-operatives; Dr Tun Lwin, Assistant Secretary, Ministry of Livestock, Fisheries and Rural Development; Dr Aung Kyaw Thin, Deputy Director General, Ministry of Education; Daw Thandar Saw, Assistant Director, Ministry of Finance; Zaw Win, Staff, Ministry of Commerce.

The policy dialogue also benefited from the insights of Club de Madrid members Prime Minister Han Seung Soo, Former Prime Minister of Korea, and President Boris Tadić, Former President of Serbia, made possible by the work of the Club de Madrid Secretariat: María Elena Agüero, Deputy Secretary General; Rubén Campos, Programs Coordinator; Veronique Andrieux, Senior Program Officer; Carla Fernández-Durán, Program Officer; Rafael Moreno, Project Officer.

Many thanks also to the ERIA delegation for their active participation in the policy dialogue: Professor Toshihiro Kudo, Professor, National Graduate Institute of Policy Studies, Japan (GRIPS); Mr Yasushi Iwata, ERIA General Manager; Mr Kyota Yamamoto, EIRA Deputy General Manager.

The Embassy of Switzerland in Myanmar/Swiss Agency for Development and Co-operation was instrumental in the third phase of the Review, providing financial support, guidance as well as active participation in the policy dialogue. Special thanks to Paul Seger, Ambassador of Switzerland to Myanmar; Peter Tschumi, Deputy Head of Mission/Head of Co-operation; Ms Carin Salerno, Counsellor, Deputy Director of Co-operation; Gentiane Huber, Programme Officer; and Nay Myo Zaw, Programme Officer.

Table of contents

Boxes

Abbreviations and acronyms

ADB	Asian Development Bank
AEC	ASEAN Economic Community
ASEAN	Association of Southeast Asian Nations
BRI	Bank Rakyat of Indonesia
CSO	Central Statistical Organization of Myanmar
DAR	Department of Agricultural Research
DBSA	Development Bank of South Africa
DICA	Directorate of Investment and Company Administration
DOA	Department of Agriculture
EIA	Environmental Impact Assessments
ERIA	Economic Research Institute for ASEAN and East Asia
FDI	Foreign Direct Investment
ICTs	Information and Communication Technologies
ISO	International Organization for Standardization
LEC	Law on Environmental Conservation
LUCs	Land Use Certificates
MADB	Myanmar Agricultural Development Bank
MDCR	Multi-dimensional Country Review
MDRI-CESD	Myanmar Development Resource Institute, Centre for Economic and Social Development
MFIs	Microfinance Institutions
MIC	Myanmar Investment Commission
MMK	Myanmar Kyat
NGOs	Non-Governmental Organisations
ODA	Official Development Assistance
OECD	Organisation for Economic Co-operation and Development
PFM	Public Financial Management
R&D	Research and Development
RML	Reuters Market Light
SEA	Strategic Environmental Assessments
SMEs	Small and Medium-sized Enterprises
SOEs	State-Owned Enterprises

SPS	Sanitary and Phytosanitary
TVET	Technical and Vocational Education and Training
UMFCCI	Union of Myanmar Federation of Chambers of Commerce and Industry
UNESCAP	United Nations Economic and Social Commission for Asia and the Pacific
UNESCO	United Nations Educational, Scientific and Cultural Organisation
VET	Vocational Education and Training
WTO	World Trade Organization
YAU	Yezin Agricultural University

Executive summary

The progress made in Myanmar since the start of its transition process in 2011 has been remarkable, particularly given the country's unique challenge of a "triple transition". In the political sphere, the country has moved from military rule to multi-party democracy; economic reforms aim to transform a largely centrally planned economy to a market-based one; and finally, negotiated ceasefires in the on-going peace process have halted several of the prolonged conflicts in the country's border areas.

In the last four years, a raft of new laws has been debated and passed by parliament. Reforms have led to greater freedoms of assembly and speech, as the flourishing private media sector attests. The telecommunications landscape has been transformed, driving down the price of a mobile phone so that it has become accessible to millions. The introduction of the foreign investment law has enabled foreign ownership of business ventures, aiming to bring in vital financial resources for development as well as modern technologies and know-how.

It will be crucial to sustain this drive in order to establish institutions that improve the conditions for development and the well-being of citizens. The general elections held in November 2015, deemed to be free and fair, marked an important milestone in this process. The number of new laws passed and visible changes in Myanmar have been impressive, yet more is needed to ensure that reforms are as deep as they are broad. Furthermore, many people, especially in rural areas, continue to live in poverty and have not yet felt the benefits of economic and political reforms.

The modernisation of Myanmar's economy starts with agriculture

Myanmar is in need of a structural transformation from an agrarian economy to one based more on a mix of modern activities, including manufacturing and services. Modernising the agricultural sector by building linkages to complementary non-agricultural activities – an "agricultural value chain" approach – could set in motion this process of structural transformation.

This path for inclusive development is particularly relevant for Myanmar because of its natural resource endowments, its strategic location and a favourable external environment. Furthermore, given Myanmar's level of economic development, its large rural population, the weight of agriculture in the economy and the number of people that are employed in agriculture, a development strategy that puts agriculture and rural development at its core has the potential to make a significant positive impact for millions.

Taking the findings and recommendations of the *Multi-dimensional Review of Myanmar* as their starting point, participants in two policy dialogue events organised for the Review structured the elements needed to pursue this development strategy into six priority fields of action:

Products and markets: Creating value through quality

Producing goods that meet market demand, including the demand for quality, will be central to the success of Myanmar's agricultural sector. The following recommendations are aimed at linking Myanmar to global agricultural chains and expanding its productive capacity beyond primary products.

- Identify more priority sectors for development and opportunities to add value to primary products
- Support producers and exporters to meet international export requirements by providing information and by expanding capacity to meet international food safety requirements, e.g. increase ISO-certified laboratories and qualified technical staff
- Proactively support the creation of the Myanmar agricultural brand
- Explore alternative organisational structures in agriculture – for example, clusters or contracting – that may foster value chains and provide greater impetus to modernisation
- Upgrade the infrastructure on which value chains and a vibrant export sector depend in the framework of the country's strategic plan on industrial and economic zones.

Education and research

Inadequate agronomic skills and knowledge are holding back Myanmar's agricultural sector and a lack of technical and vocational skills is a constraint to industrialisation. There is also a lack of research and development on improving production techniques and product quality.

- Disseminate information to farmers and rural businesses more efficiently: proposals include establishing rural training hubs for commercial smallholder farmers and agri-food SMEs; strengthening links between agricultural research institutions and extension services; and using modern communications technology (e.g. mobile phones) to deliver price information and advisory services
- Dedicate more resources to agricultural research and development, including on high-value crops
- Scale up provision of quality technical and vocational education and training (TVET) and align TVET courses and curricula with the needs of the labour market.

Modernising agricultural finance

The rural sector's limited access to credit has constrained productivity and slowed structural transformation. Participants in the policy dialogue saw the reform of the Myanmar Agricultural Development Bank (MADB) as a key measure. Yet reforming the MADB would not in itself resolve the underlying dynamics behind a lack of credit, nor could a single institution be capable of efficiently providing the full range of services needed. Better progress would be made by the overall development of financial institutions and markets, to expand the financial sector's coverage, increase the products and services on offer, and improve resource allocation. Potential actions include to:

- Develop formal financial institutions and markets supported by an appropriate regulatory and supervisory framework; resolve any conflicts of interest between the commercial and regulatory objectives of government in the financial sector

- Expand the range of financial services available to the rural economy, e.g. by providing incentives for commercial banks to operate in the agricultural sector by raising or eliminating the ceiling on bank lending rates
- Reform the MADB, dividing it into a development bank and a commercial bank and pursuing the corporatisation of the commercial entity
- Facilitate the development of securities and credit markets.

Strengthening land rights

Improved land security would raise agricultural productivity, better align production with market demand, and improve the rural sector's access to finance. Any strategy should be aimed at removing uncertainty on land rights, which currently impedes efficient resource allocation and dampens incentives to produce and invest.

- Resolve any conflict and ambiguity in the regulatory framework for land tenure and crop choice, and consider any indirect restrictions on land use (e.g. limits on loans for high-value crops).
- Complete the issuance of Land Use Certificates, help farmers understand their purpose, and monitor their acceptance as collateral by lenders

Expand the capacity to administer land laws; consider, for example, decentralising land management.

From expectation to action – participatory policy design

To be successful in the long run, any national development plan must be underpinned by a national consensus. The policy dialogue emphasised the need for the future vision for Myanmar to reflect citizens' needs and wants. To that end, participants suggested a number of actions:

- Organise public fora for dialogue between policy makers, farmers and other stakeholders
- Review existing polls, surveys that have been carried out on public expectations and preferences
- Launch new polls to ensure that citizens are regularly consulted.

It will be equally important to remove obstacles to this process, including a weak capacity to implement policy and distrust in the government, stemming from perceptions of corruption. Measures to help achieve this goal could include:

- Setting out and publishing clear criteria for policy and administrative decisions in order to reduce the ability for decision makers to exercise undue discretion
- Increasing transparency, monitoring and evaluation in the planning process.

Managing migration

Migration is deeply intertwined with the development process. Rural to urban migration is to be expected as part of structural transformation: as agriculture becomes more productive, labour is freed up to work in more productive sectors, often in urban areas. Rates of international labour emigration also tend to initially increase as countries become wealthier, before peaking and dropping again. To harness the development potential of migration, a number of policy options are available to Myanmar:

- Continue efforts to formalise migration channels, working with neighbouring governments to legalise and register workers from Myanmar

- Lower the cost of remittances, for example by increasing competition in the banking sector, to channel more financial resources to households
- Provide incentives for Myanmar workers to stay in the country by improving local labour-market conditions, rather than by imposing coercive measures to prevent emigration
- Introduce schemes to encourage the diaspora to return and contribute their skills to Myanmar.

Multi-dimensional Review of Myanmar
Volume 3. From Analysis to Action

Chapter 1

Overview: Opportunities and challenges for Myanmar

This is the third phase report of the Multi-dimensional Review of Myanmar. The first report diagnosed the constraints to development in the country across a number of dimensions (OECD, 2013). The second report then provided in-depth analysis and policy recommendations on the critical issue identified in the first phase: the need for a structural transformation of the economy (OECD, 2015).

The Review asserts that this structural transformation could be kick-started by agricultural modernisation and rural development. Furthermore, given Myanmar's level of economic development, its large rural population, the weight of agriculture in the economy and the number of people that are employed in agriculture, a development strategy that puts agriculture and rural development at its heart has the potential to significantly improve the lives of millions of people.

This third report synthesises the findings from the first two reports according to priorities defined by stakeholders in Myanmar (Figure 1.1). Using a "governmental learning spiral" approach – a technique for learning in complex political environments – participants in two policy dialogue events worked through the findings and recommendations of the earlier reports. The purpose of the policy dialogue was to transfer the knowledge embodied in the reports to local actors as a first step towards implementation.

Figure 1.1. **Multi-dimensional Review of Myanmar process**

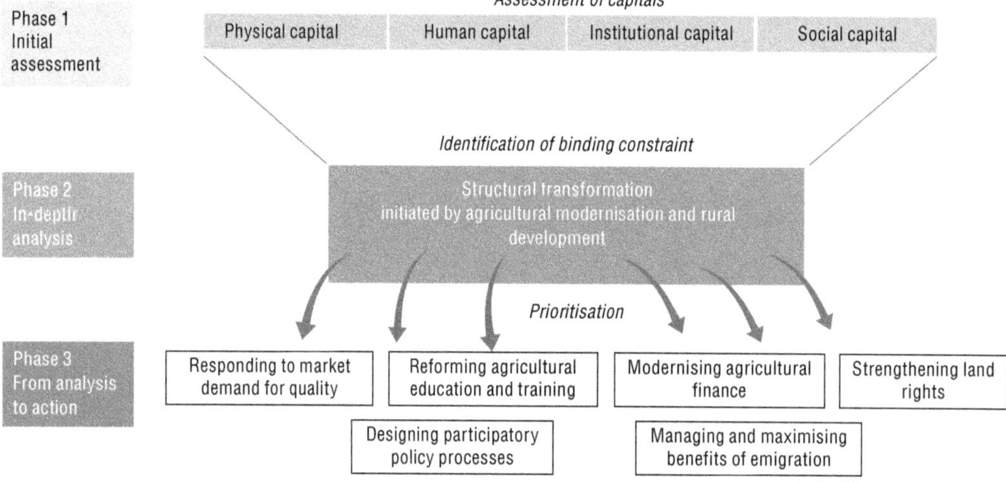

This chapter begins with an overview of the development potential of Myanmar and an assessment of well-being in the country. It then presents a stock-taking of the four capital stocks – physical, human, institutional and social – which underpin development. The next chapter then focuses on the issue of structural transformation through agricultural modernisation and rural development.

Myanmar has enormous development potential

Few countries have the opportunity to establish a robust development strategy based on assets as abundant as those possessed by Myanmar. The country has fertile land that is also rich in minerals, hydrocarbons, forests and hydro-resources, an ancient civilisation with historical sites of global importance, an advantageous geostrategic position between India and the People's Republic of China (hereafter "China"), and a relatively young population. However, these assets have not yet been fully employed to realise Myanmar's development potential, nor have the benefits they have produced been shared among the population. The country has huge latent promise.

Myanmar's rich agricultural resources made it the rice bowl of Asia a half century ago, and agriculture will need to be a key pillar of a successful multi-pronged development strategy. Large areas of fertile agricultural land are among Myanmar's major endowments, with over 0.22 hectares of arable land per person (Figure 1.2). In addition, Myanmar boasts large swathes of forested land which contain a wide variety of major commercially viable species. Nearly 47% of Myanmar's total land area is covered by forests, accounting for nearly 40% of the total forested area of Southeast Asia. Furthermore, Myanmar ranks 14th among all nations in water availability. These rich water resources provide the country with a diverse marine life and a basis for the fishing industry, and are the source of three-quarters of Myanmar's electricity. Indeed, Myanmar has huge hydropower potential in its upland border regions, estimated to be more than 100 000 megawatts.

Figure 1.2. **Arable land is abundant in Myanmar, especially in per capita terms**

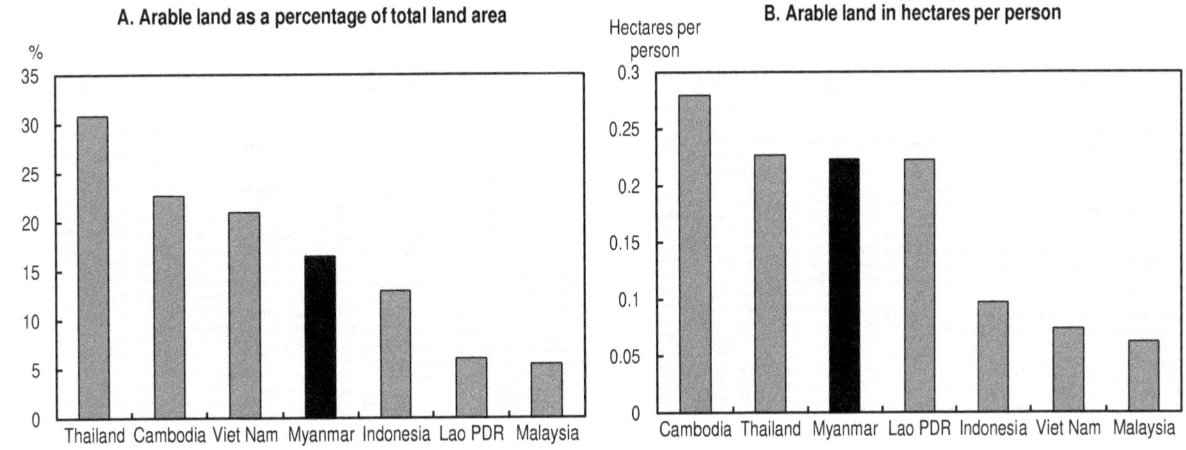

A. Arable land as a percentage of total land area

%

35
30
25
20
15
10
5
0

Thailand Cambodia Viet Nam Myanmar Indonesia Lao PDR Malaysia

B. Arable land in hectares per person

Hectares per person

0.3
0.25
0.2
0.15
0.1
0.05
0

Cambodia Thailand Myanmar Lao PDR Indonesia Viet Nam Malaysia

Source: CSO (2013), *Myanmar Data: CD-ROM 2011-12*, Central Statistical Organization, Ministry of National Planning and Economic Development, Nay Pyi Taw, Myanmar and World Bank (2013), *World Development Indicators* (database), *http://databank.worldbank.org*.

StatLink http://dx.doi.org/10.1787/888933346776

Minerals, hydrocarbons and other non-renewable natural resources are found in Myanmar in a diversity rarely seen elsewhere. The sustainable and equitable exploitation of these resources should form another pillar of the country's multi-pronged development strategy, enabling future generations to reap the benefits of these assets. Myanmar's reserves of natural gas are estimated at 410 billion cubic feet onshore and 11 trillion offshore (37th highest in the world). The country is also rich in coal, copper, gold, zinc, tungsten, precious stones, rare earth metals and other minerals. Furthermore, the geographical proximity of China and India provide Myanmar with a large and growing market for these resources. This position is enhanced by China's desire to shift energy import routes away from the vulnerable Straits of Malacca and improve their energy security through over-land supply lines (some of which will run through Myanmar).

Myanmar's geographic location is in itself an important resource. Myanmar's location between the two emerging giants of China and India and its access to the Indian Ocean via the Bay of Bengal ensures its geo-strategic importance. For its neighbours, Myanmar holds the key to increasing connectivity and the ease of trade in the region. The country forms a land bridge between South Asia and Southeast Asia and provides access to maritime trade routes in the Indian Ocean. Major infrastructure projects to improve transport links between the countries in the region are being planned or are already underway. These infrastructure projects could potentially revitalise landlocked regions in the east of India and the south west of China.

Myanmar also has a brief time window in which it can benefit significantly from its current population distribution. The country's population will keep increasing in the next couple of decades, holding potential growth rates (at which the economy can keep growing in the medium term without increasing inflationary pressures) high. The shape of Myanmar's population pyramid (vase-shaped) suggests that the increasing population in the coming decades will be contributing to high potential growth (Figure 1.3). Instead of a concave or expanding pyramidal profile such as that of many countries at similar income levels, Myanmar's population pyramid is a similar shape to that of China at the start of the 2000s when the country experienced some of its highest growth rates, with the age group of 20-24 years being the most populous.

Figure 1.3. **Increasing population in the coming decades will contribute to high potential growth**

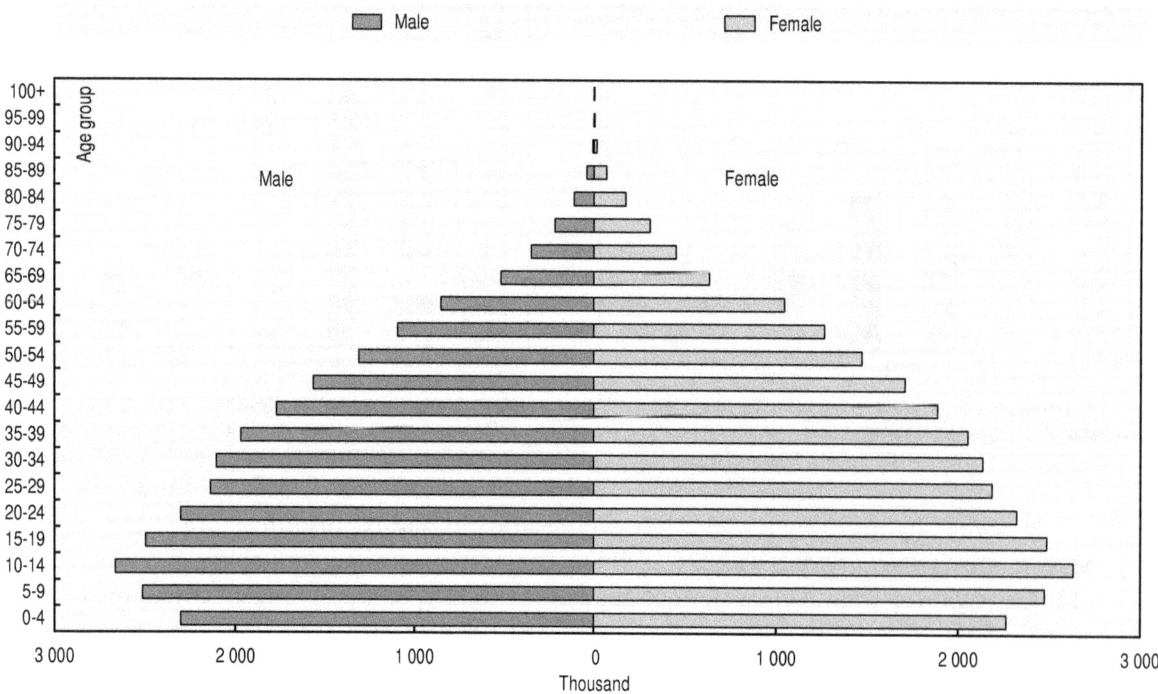

Source: United Nations (2015), *World Population Prospects: The 2015 Revision, Standard Variants* (database), *http://esa.un.org/unpd/wpp/Excel-Data/population.htm* (accessed 10 February 2016).

StatLink http://dx.doi.org/10.1787/888933346787

Well-being is undermined by low levels of social connections, empowerment and participation

Development involves more than simple improvement in incomes or other material conditions. In its broadest terms, development can be thought of as a sustainable improvement in the well-being of a country's citizens. Neglect of the broader dimensions of well-being in development policies is likely to impair their effectiveness, in part because it could lead to overlooking the social and political consensus which is indispensable for the pursuit of these goals.

This section examines indicators of well-being for Myanmar in relation to comparable indicators for other "benchmark" nations, using the OECD *How's Life?* framework (Box 1.1). The indicators for Myanmar are chosen so that they cover all of the main dimensions of well-being, are available for Myanmar, are likely to be updated in the future on a regular basis and for which comparisons can be made to other countries. These indicators form a baseline for monitoring Myanmar's development and assessing progress. They can be monitored into the future at a relatively low cost and provide a reasonably comprehensive way to assess the impacts of development across all the relevant dimensions of well-being.

Most of the benchmark nations have been selected either because they have geographical, cultural, or economic ties to Myanmar, or because they are at a similar level of economic development. These countries provide an indication of the level of outcomes in different domains of well-being that might be achievable for Myanmar and allow for the identification of areas of relative strength or weakness for Myanmar when compared to similar countries. Several other countries that are at significantly higher levels of economic development compared to Myanmar and are either direct neighbours or other members of ASEAN (Association of Southeast Asian Nations) are also included in the benchmark group to provide signposts as to possible future outcomes of the development process and to assist in assessing the gap to be closed in development outcomes.

As a developing nation, well-being is generally low in Myanmar when considered in absolute terms. This cuts across all the outcomes considered in this report. However, of greater relevance for Myanmar's development are the strengths and weaknesses of Myanmar when compared to how the country might be expected to perform given its level of economic development. In this respect the profile of Myanmar is somewhat uneven (Figure 1.4). Myanmar's human capital stock, as represented by employment, health, and education outcomes is somewhat better than might be anticipated. In addition, female outcomes are similar to, or even better than, male outcomes across most of these areas. This is consistent with a society that places a high value on education.

Measured environmental outcomes reflect Myanmar's abundant natural resources, but also suggest a slightly higher than expected run-down of the country's natural capital stocks. Given the weak link between GDP growth and improvements in environmental outcomes, this will be an important area to monitor in the future.

Offsetting Myanmar's strong natural capital stocks and positive human capital outlook, Myanmar's greatest weaknesses lie in the areas of social connections, empowerment and participation. These indicators capture social relations at the official level (reflected in perceived corruption and voicing an opinion to officials) as well as at the interpersonal level (reflected in the proportion of the population with someone to count on in an emergency) and are different measures of trust, between individuals and of individuals towards institutions, that make up social capital.

Box 1.1. **The OECD How's Life framework**

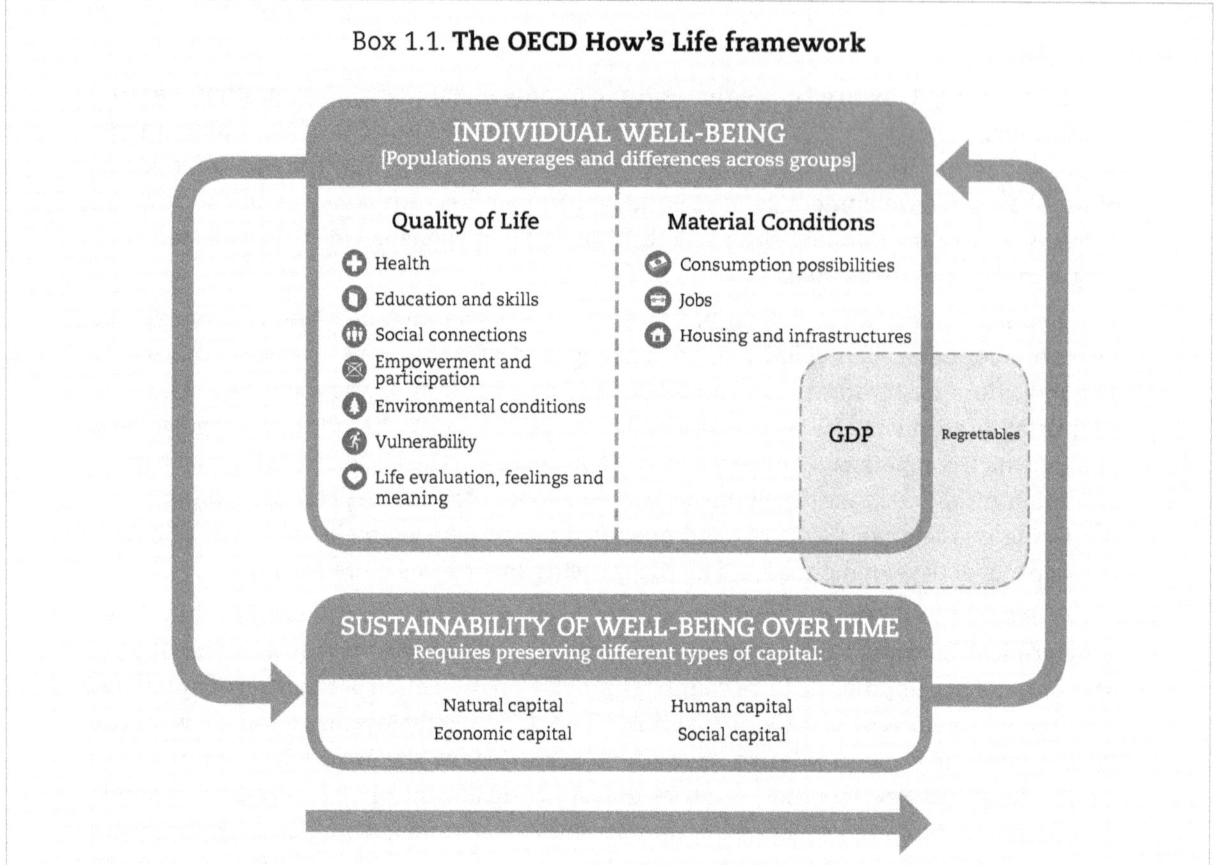

The *How's Life?* framework (OECD, 2011) was designed with developed countries in mind, but its general structure is also relevant for developing nations like Myanmar. Current well-being is described in terms of 11 dimensions covering both the material living conditions and the quality of life that people experience. These dimensions are intended to be both conceptually distinct (i.e. they capture fundamentally different aspects of well-being) and, taken collectively, comprehensive (i.e. they capture all the important aspects of well-being). Thematically, these dimensions of well-being can be seen as grounded in the capabilities that individuals have to transform resources into given ends (Sen, 1998).

While the statistical information that is currently available for Myanmar allows for only a partial application of this framework, this section provides a first, high-level review of how life is in Myanmar. Improving the statistical information on people's living conditions in Myanmar should be an important priority within the broader agenda of upgrading the statistical infrastructure of the country.

In these areas, Myanmar's performance is worse than would be expected for countries at a similar level of economic development. This suggests that outcomes in this area will represent a crucial constraint on Myanmar's development unless they are addressed, but also that proportionately large gains can be made if improvements are achieved. Furthermore, given Myanmar's transition away from military rule and its ethnically diverse population, concerted efforts to improve outcomes in social connections, empowerment and political participation will likely be important for socially sustainable development.

Figure 1.4. **Well-being in Myanmar is undermined by low social connections, empowerment and participation**

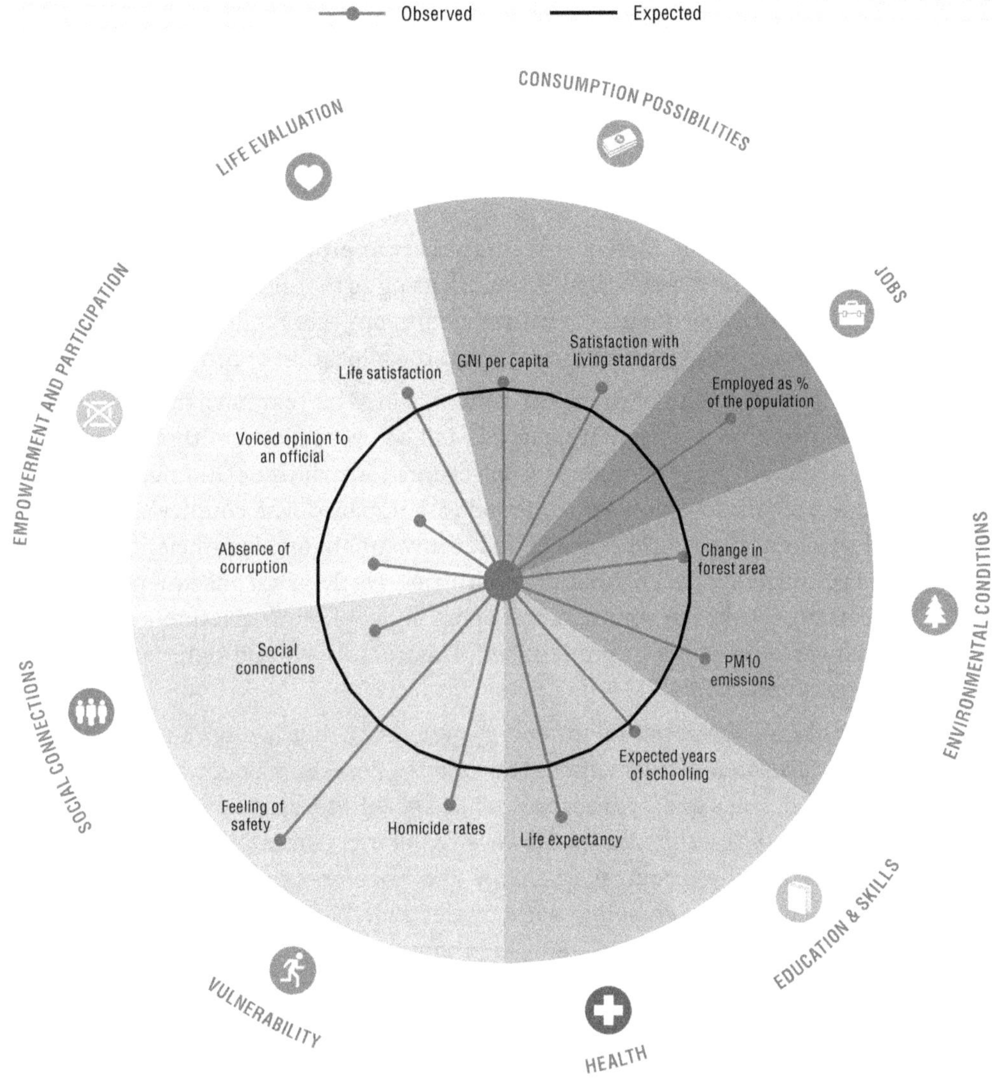

Note: The circle represents the level of well-being that could be expected in Myanmar given its level of economic development. Where the lines extend further than the circle, Myanmar's well-being outcomes are above what would be expected given its level of economic development.

Source: Authors' calculations based on Gallup Organization (2013), *Gallup World Monitor;* Transparency International (2012), *Corruption Perceptions Index 2012, www.transparency.org/research/cpi/overview* (accessed 10 March 2013); UNDP (2013), *International Human Development Indicators* (database), United Nations Development Programme, *http://hdr.undp.org/en/statistics/*; UNESCO (2013), *UNESCO Institute for Statistics Data Centre* (database), United Nations Educational, Scientific and Cultural Organization, *http://stats.uis.unesco.org/*; WHO (2013), *Global Health Observatory Data Repository* (database), World Health Organization, *http://apps.who.int/gho/data/view.main* and World Bank (2013), *World Development Indicators* (database), *http://databank.worldbank.org*.

Myanmar needs to rapidly accumulate different types of capital for structural transformation

The following analysis of the different types of capital that underpin development leads to the identification of structural transformation as the central development challenge for Myanmar. A structural transformation of Myanmar's economy would significantly improve well-being outcomes for its citizens. To realise this potential, Myanmar needs to quickly build up stocks of all types of capital, but improving institutional and social capital in particular is essential.

Physical capital

The OECD's initial assessment of Myanmar's physical capital highlighted that rapid physical capital accumulation is required to sustain the country's growth and to meet its development targets. In particular, the first report highlighted that Myanmar requires urgent upgrades and expansion of its transport networks, energy infrastructure and telecommunications systems. Moreover, the necessary improvements to infrastructure need to be supported by a more effective institutional setting as the split of responsibilities across different government departments for infrastructure projects hinders the development of overarching strategies, priority identification and the allocation of funding.

The quantity and quality of transport networks in Myanmar have improved following infrastructure investments since 2013, but still fall below the level of their regional peers. Road density and road quality remain low with some townships not connected to the road network, while a significant proportion of roads are unpaved. The country's rail network is also underdeveloped following decades of under-investment and insufficient maintenance, with limited connectivity to neighbouring countries. Partly as a consequence, waterways play an important role in the country's transport network. With aviation capabilities also below desired capacity, plans to modernise infrastructure should help facilitate greater mobility of goods and people.

Myanmar has a large potential for energy generation, but is often unable to meet the needs of its population and businesses. The country possesses latent sustainable energy sources from wind, solar and hydropower, while recent assessments have indicated that coal, gas and oil reserves are significant. However, Myanmar currently lacks the technological capabilities to exploit these sources of energy and transfer it to its people. In some areas of the country, people are completely without electricity; just 28% of the rural population has access to electricity compared to 89% in urban areas. Furthermore, in areas served by electricity, power shortages are frequent, disrupting people's everyday lives, businesses and community services. While installed capacity has been increasing, a further expansion is required, alongside improvements in transmission networks, to expand supply sufficiently for it to meet demand both in the short term and the long term.

The Multi-dimensional Country Review also demonstrated that Myanmar's telecommunications capabilities were limited in coverage and quality. Telephone (fixed and mobile) and Internet penetration were both very low in the country, with little over 10% of the population owning a mobile phone and only 2.1% of people having accessed the Internet in the last 12 months (World Bank, 2014). Restricted access and high prices of telecommunications were, in part, due to highly monopolised market structures. Since the initial assessment, there has been rapid progress in the telecoms sector, particularly in the mobile market. In addition to the state-owned Myanma Posts and Telecommunications, two foreign telecoms companies – Ooredoo and Telenor – have entered the market. An improved regulatory framework for the sector and additional competition have seen prices fall dramatically and access greatly increase.

Human capital

Sustainable economic development in Myanmar is conditional on the availability and quality of the country's human capital. Significant progress in improving access to and the quality of education has been made since 1990, particularly in improving literacy rates to a level comparable with the region's middle-income economics (China, the Philippines and Thailand), but further improvements in the education system will be required if Myanmar is to accumulate the necessary skills to aid the country's development and concurrent movement up the value chain. A stronger focus on vocational training and a higher proportion of tertiary graduates in education and health will be essential, and overall spending on education at all levels needs to be boosted to address the challenges ahead.

Myanmar is at the doorstep of broad-based access to basic education, but greater expenditure is required to meet the country's needs. Initiatives to increase access to basic education have been successful with a high formal primary intake (98.5% in 2011) and a drastically improved survival rate to the last grade of primary since 1999. However, educational attainment does not go far beyond the most fundamental literacy skills. With compulsory school years being limited to ages 5-9, only 69% of children finish the last grade of primary school and gross enrolment rates for lower and upper secondary education, at 62% and 32% in 2010, respectively, are significantly lower than their regional middle-income country peers. In a positive development since the initial assessment, lower secondary school has now been made free and compulsory. For there to be sustainable provision of basic education for all, a well-thought increase in government spending on education will be required. In 2011, Myanmar's public expenditure totalled 0.8% of GDP, in comparison to a 3.7% average across regional peers (Figure 1.5). Since the MDCR initial assessment was published, education expenditure has increased, although further resources are needed. In the medium term, expenditure could also be rebalanced towards secondary (including vocational) and tertiary education to meet the country's needs.

Figure 1.5. **Public expenditure on education is low in Myanmar**

Public expenditure on education as percentage of GDP in Myanmar compared to its peers, 2011

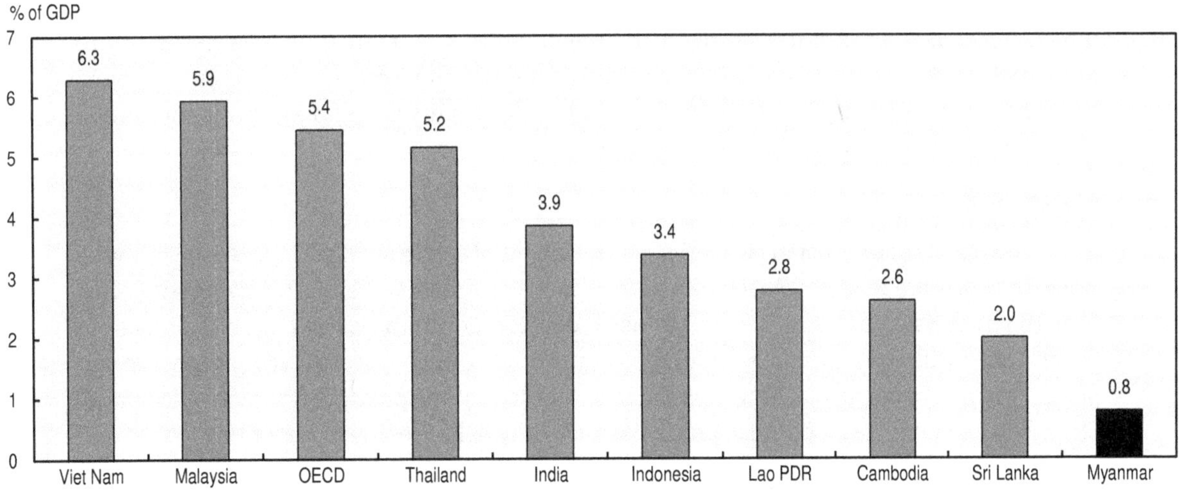

Note: The figure for Myanmar is based on 2011 data. The OECD average is based on 2011 data (excluding Greece, Korea, Luxembourg and Turkey). The figures for Cambodia, Lao PDR and Viet Nam are based on 2010 data.

Source: World Bank (2016), *World Development Indicators* (database), *http://databank.worldbank.org*, accessed 10 February 2016.

StatLink http://dx.doi.org/10.1787/888933346790

Further improvements in the quality and type of tertiary education provided will be necessary to support the transformation of the Myanmar economy. This lack of skills has often been a stumbling block for low- and middle-income countries attempting to move up the value chain. Substantial steps have been made, particularly in the quantity of education available; the number of higher education institutions increased from 32 in 1988 to 164 in 2012, with a fourfold increase in higher education students over the same period to approximately 500 000. However, as future demand shifts, the supply and quality of skills of Myanmar's workforce must adjust to reflect this. In particular, the specialisation mix of graduates in tertiary education should be analysed to ensure that the economy is not lacking skills in education and health – sectors that improve human capital – and that sufficient management and entrepreneurial capabilities exist to encourage the growth of a vibrant business sector. An industrialising Myanmar will also need strong mid-level technical and vocational skills. Efforts to increase access to vocational education should be enhanced in the short run, but in the medium term a sophisticated and formal apprenticeship programme as is apparent in Switzerland might be a consideration for Myanmar.

However, to better identify future skill demand in Myanmar, the co-ordination of the education system between ministries needs to be improved. Inefficiencies and potential misallocation of educational resources must be limited by minimising the number of responsible ministries. Ideally, only one ministry would be responsible for the provision and quality of education at all levels. This ministry would thus be responsible for co-ordinating a strategy for profession-specific education that incorporates the views of the private sector, and an analysis of the labour market to examine where unemployment is concentrated and how salaries in different sectors (including public vs. private sector) compare, among each other and with other countries.

Myanmar's demographic challenge makes improving educational attainment and aligning skills provision to the economy's requirements extremely time sensitive. Myanmar's population will keep increasing in the next couple of decades, holding potential growth rates high, but the structure of the population shows that it will face ageing earlier than other countries in the region with similar income levels (Figure 1.6). Therefore, this flux of entrants into the labour market must be given the opportunities to learn the skills necessary to participate in the economy and help the country fully exploit its growth momentum to avoid getting old before getting rich. Changes to policy responsibility and strategy implementation must thus be enacted quickly and effectively.

Social capital

Social capital, and trust in particular, will be essential to sustain Myanmar's development. However, there are relatively low levels of trust in government and other formal institutions. This mistrust risks undermining an inclusive development process as the level of trust in government will affect people's willingness to take part in co-operative action and accept policy reforms. In particular, limitations on the freedom of the press, civil society and spaces for public debate mean these institutions cannot fully hold the Government to account and ensure transparency and accountability, essential elements in trust-building. Trust is not completely lacking in the country, however, as proven by the *hundi* system of informal money transfer which functions thanks to high levels of interpersonal trust. Furthermore, people's confidence in religious institutions is very high in Myanmar; in a 2012 poll, 96% of respondents said they had confidence in religious organisations, the second highest rate in Southeast Asia.

Figure 1.6. **Myanmar's population will start ageing soon**

Share of age group 10-64 in total population

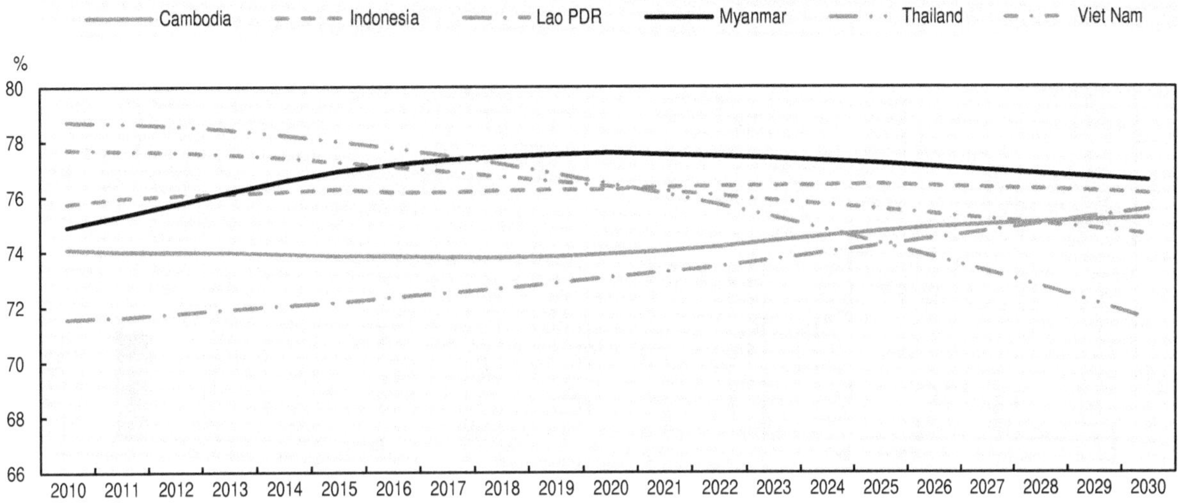

Source: United Nations (2015), *World Population Prospects: The 2015 Revision, Standard Variants* (database), *http://esa.un.org/unpd/wpp/Excel-Data/population.htm* (accessed 10 February 2016).

StatLink http://dx.doi.org/10.1787/888933346806

Historically, there has been a general lack of trust in the government's intentions to act in the wider public interest. Poor quality or, in some areas, non-existent public service delivery is a result of inadequate government spending and persistent corruption. High-level corruption in the form of cronyism and nepotism is compounded by low-level corruption that affects people's everyday lives in Myanmar (Figure 1.7). Businesses and individuals are regularly faced with corruption, and a lack of standardised procedures and fees, for example in customs valuation, opens up opportunities for petty corruption. Public officials in a position to grant permissions thus have the opportunity to abuse their power for personal gain with little fear of sanction. However, the government has stepped up its efforts to fight corruption through reforms that aim to achieve good governance and clean government.

The lack of trust extends to other institutions in the country which are associated with the government. In a 2012 poll, just 52% of respondents in Myanmar said they had confidence in the judicial system and the courts, largely due to the heavy influence of the executive and the military and the lengthy duration of court procedures. While the new constitution officially separates these powers, the executive is still thought to wield too much influence over the judiciary. As a response, the Supreme Court established a three-year plan (2015-17) focusing on five areas: public access; public awareness; judiciary independence and accountability; equality, fairness and integrity of the judiciary; and efficiency and timeliness of case processing, with quantified performance targets.

The political reforms which spearheaded the country's recent transition are helping to improve trust, although the progress is fragile. This has been reflected in improvements in international indices such as the Economist Intelligence Unit's Democracy Index (up one-third between 2006 and 2012. Yet progress must be maintained and reinforced; Freedom House still classified Myanmar as "not free" at the time of the initial assessment. The general elections in November 2015, judged to be free and fair according to international observers, were an important milestone in the process of building trust in the political reforms and the transition to democracy.

Figure 1.7. **Corruption is common in Myanmar**

Corruption Perceptions Index 2015

Country	Score
OECD average	70
Malaysia	50
Thailand	38
India	38
China	37
Indonesia	36
Philippines	35
Viet Nam	31
Nepal	27
Bangladesh	25
Lao PDR	25
Myanmar	22
Cambodia	21

Note: A lower Corruption Perceptions Index score stands for higher levels of corruption in a country.

Source: Transparency International (2016), *Corruption Perceptions Index 2015*, *www.transparency.org/cpi2015* (accessed 10 February 2016).

StatLink http://dx.doi.org/10.1787/888933346815

The introduction of a largely civilian parliament in 2011 appears to be a genuine forum for debate, helping strengthen the political voice of the country's different states and regions, ethnic groups and opposition parties. Furthermore, trust has been boosted by the absence of cases in which parliamentarians have been targeted for being critical of government policy, and the process by which the legislative by-elections were held in 2012. However, while progress in political reforms has so far been promising, there is still some way to go towards true political inclusion and representation, particularly given the strong presence of the military and the under-representation of women in parliament. Amending the constitutional guarantee that provides the military with 25% of all seats in the parliament will be of high importance, as it currently enables the military to veto any amendments.

Mechanisms to ensure transparency and accountability, vital to generating trust between citizens and their government, have been restricted in Myanmar for a number of years. A free press, the ability of people to freely organise themselves, and in general an atmosphere of critical public debate without fear of reprisal have been largely absent, although recent reforms have brought about improvements. Formal non-state organisations, including cultural associations or religious organisations which carried out social programmes, faced difficulties in operating under the previous regime.

Civil society in Myanmar still faces obstacles, but the situation looks set to improve under the current reforms. Previously lengthy registration processes have been reduced thanks to a relaxation in legal requirements, and should enable greater growth of civil society groups. These organisations can make a difference to the country's development by providing vital social and community development services, and a stronger civil society will also help empower ethnic groups which have suffered from exclusion in the past.

The country's media is now much freer, although progress is still needed. Myanmar's constitution provides for freedom of expression and freedom of the press, and the climate for media has been gradually improving under the reform process. A number of journalists' organisations have been established which aim to participate in building the legislative framework for media in the country (Reporters without Borders, 2012), helping with the removal of censorship of print publications, and the publication of privately-owned dailies from April 2013. However, other laws restricting freedom of expression are still in place, which mean that journalists do not have the necessary legal protection to enable them to hold the government to account. Reporting on the conflicts in border areas is also limited and journalists confront problems in accessing the areas due to reporting restrictions imposed by the government.

Positive steps have been taken to increase the opportunity for people in Myanmar to participate in public debate and political dialogue. The Peaceful Gathering and Demonstration Law, introduced in December 2011, that allows citizens to hold peaceful protests is a significant step forward. However, Human Rights Watch (2012) commented that this law still imposes a series of measures which are restrictive of peaceful public assembly. This is necessary as public protest is one of the few channels that allow the people of Myanmar to express their opinions. Indeed, public consultations with local communities are infrequent and a culture of dialogue between authorities and local communities is under-developed (SiuSue, 2012) (Figure 1.8).

Figure 1.8. **Few people voice their opinion to a public official in Myanmar**

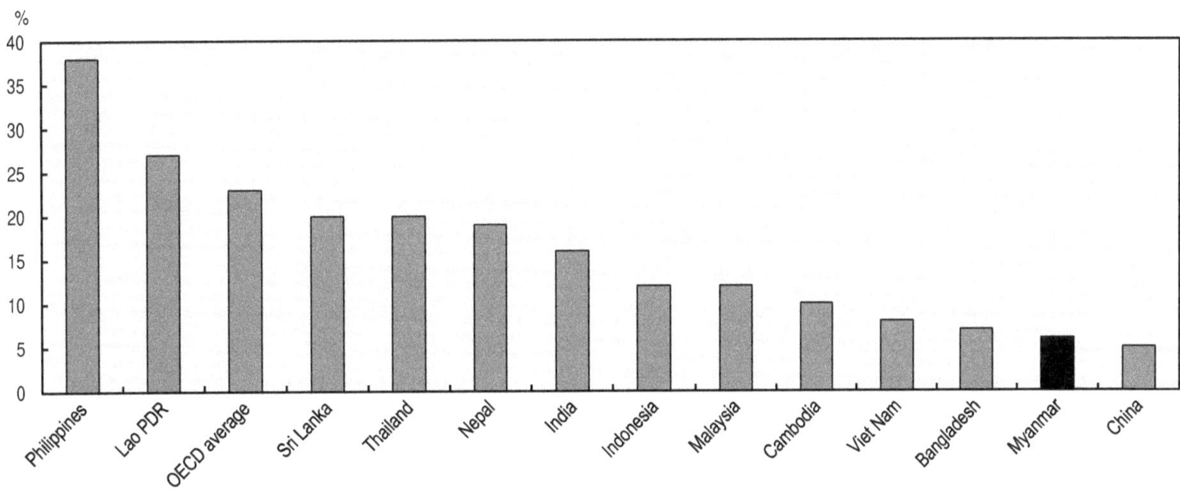

Note: The OECD average is the average of the 34 member countries of the OECD. All data are from 2012 except for the OECD countries of Chile, Germany, Japan, Mexico, Korea and United Kingdom which are from 2010.

Source: Gallup Organization (2013), *Gallup World Monitor*.

StatLink http://dx.doi.org/10.1787/888933346820

Institutional capital

Institutional capital is perhaps the most crucial of all the major forms of capital in Myanmar as it is essential to accelerate the formation of the other types of capital. The accession to power of a new government regime committed to bringing about a democratic political system offers the opportunity for a fresh start in shaping institutions, but well-designed institutional structures will not be successful if people do not trust them. Four areas stand out for building up institutional capital: ensuring the rule of law; improving the institutions governing macroeconomic and fiscal stability; the development of the private sector; and the integration of environmental policies into public policy frameworks.

The rule of law: Ensuring that both the government and the people of Myanmar are bound by the rule of law is crucial in order to build the institutional and social capital essential for the country's sustainable development. The lack of rule of law in some parts of the country has impeded government provision of major public goods such as security, justice and other services. Moreover, it has contributed to the rapid and often uncontrolled depletion of the nation's natural wealth. These problems reflect the fact that for much of the recent past, the law has not been supreme, allowing the government and powerful individuals to exercise arbitrary power, sometimes at the expense of the public good.

Reform efforts to strengthen the rule of law and overhaul key legislation are proceeding, but momentum must be maintained. While the legislative power has been handed over to a parliament with elected deputies that have been active in exercising their power, the separation of the executive and judicial powers has been less effective and the independence of the judiciary is compromised. Furthermore, the rapid pace at which new laws are passed makes it necessary that consistency among the different laws should be analysed.

Macroeconomic and financial stability: Securing macroeconomic and financial stability is essential for Myanmar as these provide the foundation for savings and investment that will facilitate sustainable long-term growth. Several episodes of macroeconomic instability have hampered Myanmar's economic development in the past decade, including a damaging banking crisis and bouts of near-hyperinflation. Hence, the authorities have rightly given high priority to creating a more effective framework for macroeconomic stabilisation that is underpinned by the establishment of a sound financial system. However, this process will be challenging given the high levels of informality, limited capacity of institutions, and the necessary sequencing of reforms.

Analysis highlighted three areas of policy in urgent need of reform. First, the financial system of the country needs to be reformed and expanded so as to be ready for the opening up of the economy to international financial and investment inflows and to be able to channel these flows to the most productive uses. Second, the frameworks, institutions and technical infrastructure for effective monetary and exchange rate policies need to be set up to sustain macroeconomic stability and to deal with external and internal shocks to the economy. And finally, a framework and the capabilities to implement fiscal policy – including budget allocation, tax policy and public debt management – have also to be developed. The overarching requirement for these reforms to succeed is that steady progress is made in returning economic activities to the formal economy so that they can be influenced by the financial system and macroeconomic policies.

Having a sound fiscal policy framework will be crucial for ensuring macroeconomic stability in Myanmar. Efforts to maintain a constant fiscal deficit will be required to keep the confidence of international markets. Therefore, to facilitate the increase in public expenditure necessary for equitable and sustainable development, a broader and deeper tax base will be required (Figure 1.9). Abolition of the dual exchange rate system may aid these efforts, but continuing reforms and enhancement of the capabilities of the tax administration are arguably of greater priority. Going forwards, an examination of whether a value-added tax would raise significant revenue should be examined.

Enabling Environment for the Private Sector: The business sector could become a driving force of Myanmar's economic development provided that an institutional framework that is conducive to entrepreneurship and private initiatives is put in place. While foreign direct investment (FDI) is needed to acquire technology, domestic private initiatives are equally important in paving the way for industrialisation. Businesses produce and supply value-added through goods and services to society while developing technology, creating jobs and generating incomes. However, business surveys have identified significant impediments to business in Myanmar, including common problems with: access to capital and credit; poor trade facilitation and high customs related fees; cumbersome business and trade licensing and permits; shortages of electricity; and weak telecommunications and inefficient transportations systems.

Figure 1.9. **Myanmar's government revenue is lower than would be expected for its income level**

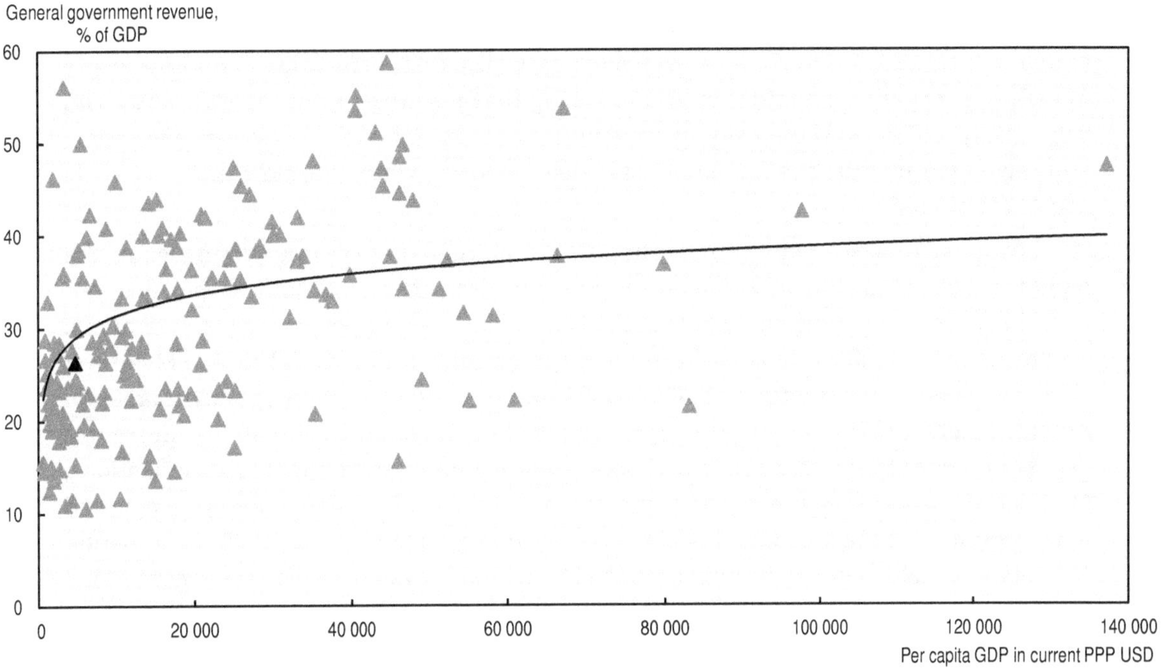

General government revenue, % of GDP

Per capita GDP in current PPP USD

Note: The black triangle represents Myanmar. The y axis is limited to 60% to improve the readability of the figure. The countries that have general government revenue more than 60% of GDP are Kiribati, Kuwait, Lesotho, Micronesia and Tuvalu.

Source: IMF (2015), *World Economic Outlook* (database), International Monetary Fund.

StatLink http://dx.doi.org/10.1787/888933346832

The establishment of a robust legal and regulatory framework for business is an urgent priority. The current structure is fragmented, with no effective centralised administrative system which includes registration or licensing for all business establishments. The government must provide a level playing field for business competition, which is a prerequisite for inclusive and sustainable development in Myanmar. The current legal and regulatory framework has a large number of deficiencies that need to be fixed in order to turn the business sector into a driver of development.

Since the initial assessment was published, the Myanmar Investment Commission (MIC) has been devising ways to improve conditions for business. Since May 2015 the MIC has been drawing up the Myanmar Private Sector Development Framework and Action Plan in collaboration with the Asian Development Bank (ADB) and drawing on a number of consultation meetings. Pillar 1 of the five-pillar plan is "Improving the Legal and Regulatory Environment". The other pillars are: Ensuring Access to Finance; Promoting Trade and Investment; Restructuring the State's Role in Business, Enterprise and Service Delivery; and

Building Myanmar's Human Capital Base. At the time of writing, the framework was due to be finalised in March 2016. Furthermore, the Directorate of Investment and Company Administration (DICA) is amending the Myanmar Companies Act (1914) into Myanmar Companies Law in order to be in line with international standards and include more provisions for liberalisation than the old law.

Environmentally Sustainable Policies: Setting up the institutional framework for effective conservation and sustainable exploitation of Myanmar's natural resources will be key to the country's development goal of becoming a middle-income country over the next two decades. Myanmar's exceptionally diverse and rich forest, land, water and mineral resources have been the main support to the domestic economy and will continue to be of major importance as the economy diversifies. However, Myanmar's natural resource endowment presents challenges and risks as well as opportunities. Avoiding costly mistakes in resource exploitation and ensuring that resources are used efficiently and sustainably will depend critically upon skilful development of the organisational, legal, and regulatory institutions for sustainable development, which are now in a very early stage of development.

Myanmar must be wary of repeating the same mistakes of other countries in the region in not integrating environmental policies with other development policies, not ensuring adequate provisions such that the traditionally strong government departments do not dominate policy debates. To inform discussion at ministerial levels, Myanmar should consider using Environmental Impact Assessments (EIA) or Strategic Environmental Assessments (SEA), to identify the effect policies will have on sustainability. Currently, depending on the business, a variety of assessments (e.g. initial environmental examinations, EIAs, social impact assessments and environmental management plan reports) are required to be submitted to the Myanmar Investment Commission. The New Law on Environmental Conservation (LEC) has significantly improved Myanmar's legal framework and institutions for environmental policy, but amendments to existing laws may be required if the framework is to be effectively implemented. In particular, a law on EIAs and SEAs will be needed to actualise the LEC provisions on these policies.

Non-government actors – local communities, NGOs and businesses – are a major resource that if effectively mobilised can greatly increase the chances that Myanmar's sustainable development objectives will be achieved. Effective involvement of these actors is likely to require support from the government to encourage their involvement, and could be facilitated through a National Council on Sustainable Development as in the Philippines.

References

CSO (2013), *Myanmar Data: CD-ROM 2011-12*, Central Statistical Organization, Ministry of National Planning and Economic Development, Nay Pyi Taw, Myanmar.

Gallup Organization (2013), *Gallup World Monitor*.

Human Rights Watch (2012), *Press Release: "Burma: New law on demonstrations falls short"*, 15 March 2012, *www.hrw.org/news/2012/03/15/burma-new-law-demonstrations-falls-short* (accessed 4 March 2013).

IMF (2015), *World Economic Outlook* (database), International Monetary Fund.

OECD (2015), *Multi-dimensional Review of Myanmar: Volume 2. In-depth Analysis and Recommendations*, OECD Development Pathways, OECD Publishing, Paris, *http://dx.doi.org/10.1787/9789264220577-en*.

OECD (2013), *Multi-dimensional Review of Myanmar: Volume 1. Initial Assessment*, OECD Development Pathways, OECD Publishing, Paris, *http://dx.doi.org/10.1787/9789264202085-en*.

OECD (2011), *How's Life? Measuring Well-being*, OECD Publishing, Paris, *http://dx.doi.org/10.1787/9789264121164-en*.

Reporters without Borders (2012), *Burmese Media Spring*, December 2012, *http://en.rsf.org/IMG/pdf/rsf_rapport_birmanie-gb-bd_2_.pdf*.

Sen, A. (1998), *Development as Freedom*, Oxford University Press.

SiuSue, M. (2012), "How civil society can engage with policy making in Myanmar's transitional context", *Colombia Journal of International Affairs*, *http://jia.sipa.columbia.edu/how-civil-society-can-engagepolicy-making-myanmar%E2%80%99s-transitional-context* (accessed 6 March 2013).

Transparency International (2016), *Corruption Perceptions Index 2015*, *www.transparency.org/cpi2015* (accessed 10 February 2016).

Transparency International (2012), *Corruption Perceptions Index 2012*, *www.transparency.org/research/cpi/overview* (accessed 10 March 2013).

UNDP (2013), *International Human Development Indicators* (database), United Nations Development Programme, *http://hdr.undp.org/en/statistics/*.

UNESCO (2013), *UNESCO Institute for Statistics Data Centre* (database), United Nations Educational, Scientific and Cultural Organization, *http://stats.uis.unesco.org/*.

United Nations (2015), *World Population Prospects, the 2015 Revision: Standard Variants* (database), *http://esa.un.org/unpd/wpp/Excel-Data/population.htm* (accessed 10 February 2016).

WHO (2013), *Global Health Observatory Data Repository* (database), World Health Organization, *http://apps.who.int/gho/data/view.main*.

World Bank (2016), *World Development Indicators* (database), *http://databank.worldbank.org* (accessed 10 February 2016).

World Bank (2013), *World Development Indicators* (database), *http://databank.worldbank.org*.

World Bank (2012), *Logistics Performance Index: Connecting to Compete 2012*, *http://lpisurvey.worldbank.org/domestic/performance* (accessed 27 April 2013).

Multi-dimensional Review of Myanmar
Volume 3. From Analysis to Action

Chapter 2

Myanmar's structural transformation starts with agricultural modernisation and rural development

Myanmar is in need of a structural transformation from an agrarian economy to one based more on a mix of modern activities, including manufacturing and services. Countries that have achieved structural transformation towards a modern economy show that broad-based agricultural transformation has been a prerequisite and catalyst for industrial development. In China and Viet Nam, for example, agricultural growth was the initial catalyst for modernising the wider economy and reducing poverty wholescale. Agricultural modernisation a) provides affordable food, b) drives up incomes of farmers enabling them to become consumers of industrial goods and services, and c) frees up labour for industrial and urban jobs and savings for investments. Kick-starting Myanmar's structural transformation therefore depends on modernising agriculture and reaping the opportunities offered by neighbouring markets for food products. With the right support and the agricultural "engine" in place, manufacturing and services can become the sustainable drivers of Myanmar's growth.

Modernising the agricultural sector by building linkages to complementary non-agricultural activities – an "agricultural value chain" approach – could set in motion this process of structural transformation. The value chain refers to the whole range of goods and services necessary for an agricultural product to move from the farm to the final consumer, such as cleaning, sorting, processing, packaging and trading. This path for development is particularly relevant for Myanmar because of its natural resource endowments, its strategic location and a favourable external environment.

Furthermore, given Myanmar's level of economic development, its large rural population, the weight of agriculture in the economy and the number of people that are employed in agriculture, a development strategy that puts agriculture and rural development at its core has the potential to make a significant positive impact for millions of people. The potential benefits could be maximised if the economic development strategy proposed here were combined with a parallel and complementary strategy to improve the delivery of public and private social services to rural populations. This includes health services, education and social protection.

Given that agricultural modernisation and rural development can be the first step in structural transformation, the policy dialogue events held for the final phase of the Multi-dimensional Review of Myanmar focused on these issues. The previous report (*Multi-dimensional Review of Myanmar Volume 2: In-depth Analysis and Recommendations*) gives more detailed analysis and recommendations on developing the manufacturing and service sectors (OECD, 2015a).

The third phase of the Review was used to prioritise policy recommendations for agricultural modernisation and rural development as a first step towards strategy-building and implementation. It applied a "governmental learning spiral" methodology to two policy dialogue events held in Yangon and Nay Pyi Taw. The governmental learning spiral approach is a concept for organising learning events in complex political environments and follows eight defined steps (Blindenbacher, 2010).

The first three steps – conceptualisation, triangulation and accommodation – take place before the learning events themselves. During these stages, the specific governance challenge is defined (in this case, Myanmar's economic modernisation starting with agriculture), existing knowledge on the topic is framed, participants are selected and invited, and trust is established between the learning actors and the knowledge broker.

During the event, the internalisation, externalisation, reconceptualisation and transformation stages take place, through which learning actors review and adapt new knowledge. The knowledge frame and starting point for the first policy dialogue event in Yangon comprised three primary sources. First, the findings and recommendations from the Volume 2 report of the Multi-dimensional Review of Myanmar. Second, the lessons from other countries' development experiences shared by former heads of state, Prime Minister Han of Korea and President Tadić of Serbia. And third, a development vision for Myanmar prepared by Jakarta-based think tank ERIA (Economic Research Institute for ASEAN and East Asia).

After the event, the configuration stage takes place, where the knowledge acquired during the event is made available and accessible to everyone involved in the event as well as to a wider audience. This present report is the output of this configuration stage and can serve as a knowledge frame for the next iteration of dialogue and learning.

The events, moderated by a "knowledge broker", convened a broad range of stakeholders in Myanmar representing different perspectives, including government officials, private sector, academics, political parties and civil society. Participants identified six priority themes and related ideas for action during the dialogue:

- Market drive – creating value through quality products
- Research and rural training for the 21st century
- Modernising agricultural finance
- Strengthening land rights
- From expectation to action – moving towards participatory policy design
- Managing migration and structural transformation

The following sections take each of these themes in turn and synthesise the relevant findings and recommendations of the Review, as well as the ideas for action developed by participants in the events.

Market drive – creating value through quality products

Given the importance of agriculture to Myanmar's structural transformation, the policy dialogue confirmed that developing agricultural value chains should be a key component of its development strategy. This approach, which examines the goods, services and conditions necessary to move a product from the agricultural producer to the consumer, should expand and deepen the links between Myanmar's agricultural, manufacturing and services sectors, as well as its links to trading partners. Export markets should be a focus for these value chains due to Myanmar's natural endowments, strategic location, membership of supranational organisations (e.g. WTO, ASEAN) and strong world demand for high-value agri-food products.

Participants emphasised the importance of producing output that is driven by market demand, including the demand for quality. There is considerable scope for this strategy to be implemented given Myanmar's current exports, which are limited to a few products and markets. The following recommendations are aimed at linking Myanmar to global agricultural chains and expanding its productive capacity beyond primary products.

Better understand the demand for Myanmar's products

Identify more priority sectors for development and opportunities to add value to primary products

A strategy to diversify Myanmar's products can help avoid market risks. Myanmar's agricultural crop sector exports are concentrated on a limited number of products, with pulses, rice and rubber accounting for 65%, 16% and 13% respectively of total crop export value (Figure 2.1). Pulses are typically exported as generic products and to a limited number of market destinations, so they may be subject to greater market risks in terms of price and quantity fluctuations than quality-differentiated products. For example, nearly 70% of pulses are exported to India to fill a production gap which can vary with India's own production or with supplies from new market entrants.

Figure 2.1. **Pulses are Myanmar's most valuable export crops**

Export shares of Myanmar's main agricultural crops, 2010/11 (% of crop export value)

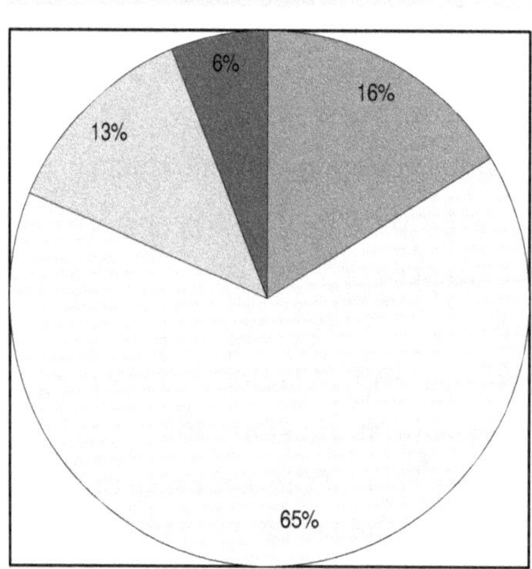

Source: CSO (2013), *Myanmar Data: CD-ROM 2011-12*, Central Statistical Organization, Ministry of National Planning and Economic Development, Nay Pyi Taw, Myanmar.

StatLink http://dx.doi.org/10.1787/888933346844

Adding value (through processing) and diversifying market destinations should be considered a strategy applicable to all products from rice to rubber. Particularly important will be to identify opportunities for smallholders to produce high-value products (e.g. crustaceans, mangos) and where production is already widespread but quality could be improved (e.g. rice). This could be incorporated into the National Export Strategy.

Help raise agricultural productivity by encouraging mechanisation and larger farms

An analysis of rice productivity by farm size indicates that both increasing farm size and mechanisation can raise labour productivity and thus incomes (Figure 2.2). The government should continue to support initiatives to increase farmers' access to machinery, including those from the Mechanised Farming Co-operatives Society and the Myanmar Rice Federation, particularly their plans for the development of Farmer Services Centres. But increases in productivity alone may not be sufficient to compensate for small farm size and incomes risk remaining low.

Figure 2.2. **The marginal products on inputs tend to increase with farm size**

Average marginal product in tonnes, by farm size

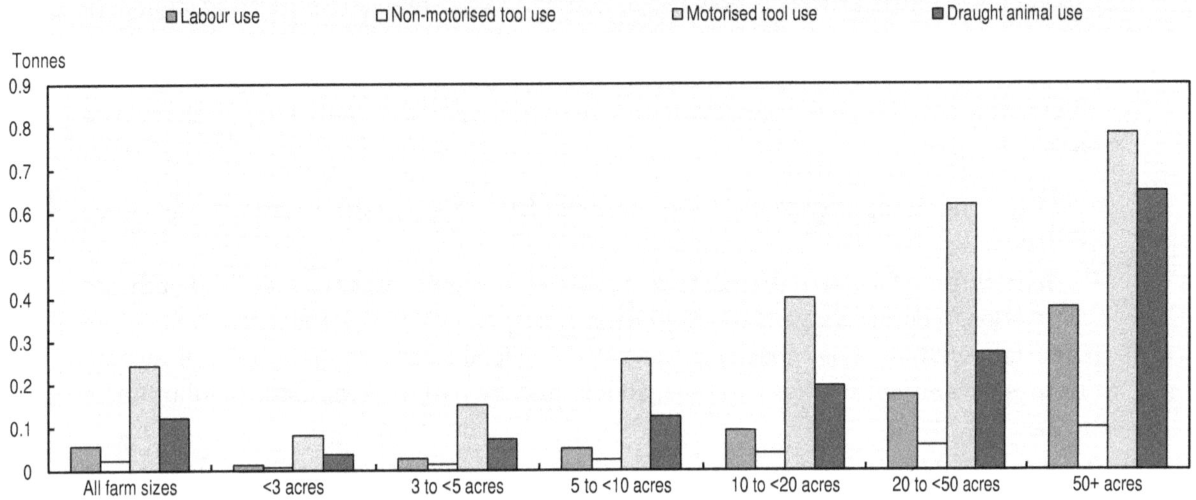

Labour use
Non-motorised tool use
Motorised tool use
Draught animal use
Tonnes
0.9
0.8
0.7
0.6
0.5
0.4
0.3
0.2
0.1
0
All farm sizes
<3 acres
3 to <5 acres
5 to <10 acres
10 to <20 acres
20 to <50 acres
50+ acres

Source: Authors' calculations, using MOAI (2013), *Report on Myanmar Census of Agriculture 2010*, Nay Pyi Taw, Myanmar.

StatLink http://dx.doi.org/10.1787/888933346852

Increasing productivity will require improvement in seed quality and increased use of fertiliser and pesticides. The government could co-ordinate and facilitate the search for a sustainable supply of quality seeds through the development of a seed bank, and source fertiliser and pesticides that meet international standards.

Support producers and exporters to meet international export requirements

As well as knowing where the potential demand is for products, producers and exporters need to ensure that Myanmar's products meet the quality and safety standards of international markets. Products of low quality are limited to market destinations that pay low prices. Products that do not meet food safety requirements will be shut out of markets altogether. For example, knowing of Myanmar farmers' excess use of pesticides or use of illegal pesticides, traders do not even attempt to enter many export markets. The government can facilitate market access by both providing information and putting in place the necessary infrastructure and systems.

Improve the delivery of information critical to production and marketing success

Facilitating contacts with new markets to promote Myanmar's agri-food products through public and private collaboration should be on the agricultural trade policy agenda. Myanmar's trade associations rely largely on their own initiatives and financing to identify new markets and to be informed of regulations and export opportunities.

The government (e.g. through the Department of Trade Promotion) could establish a centralised source of information on importing countries' requirements, such as food safety regulations as well as market information to facilitate trade, ranging from tariffs and tariff quotas to rules of origin. This information could be disseminated to regional trade centres, which could directly inform farmers and other producers through information centres, such as the rural training hubs proposed in the next section on education and research. These centres could also assist in delivering weather warnings and market price data to producers.

Promote industry associations

Industry associations can bring together producers and farmers to discuss strategies and market opportunities as well as how to overcome the scale problem in meeting standards while remaining competitive. Industry associations are also necessary as interlocutors for government and to help co-ordinate support. Promoting producer and industry associations can build the social capital necessary for furthering co-operation in meeting challenges of the sector.

Build Myanmar's capacity to meet international food safety requirements of importing countries

Satisfying the food safety regulatory requirements of ASEAN (Association of Southeast Asian Nations) countries should be a priority in anticipation of the establishment of the free trade regime. But building capacity to meet evolving food safety standards of high-income countries, given their market potential, should also be part of Myanmar's medium-term strategy.

This should include devoting resources to increase ISO-certified laboratories and appropriately qualified technical staff. A sustainable certification scheme (including inspection and testing to international standards) would need to be implemented at the same time, potentially through public-private partnerships, with the government retaining oversight of standards. A nominal fee-based certification service could be introduced to provide policy makers with information on where needs are.

Ensuring food safety compliance is not easy, particularly when traditional smallholders are to be integrated into evolving markets as experience from Viet Nam indicates (Box 2.1).

Box 2.1. **Improving food safety: Learning from Viet Nam's dragon fruit experience**

Efforts to improve smallholder access to export markets for Dragon fruit involved upgrading production methods so as to meet regulatory Sanitary and Phytosanitary (SPS) requirements and private standards, such as GLOBALG.A.P. (Global Good Agricultural Practices). Local government, agricultural services and several donors collaborated in upgrading production quality of dragon fruit to meet market demands. Food safety practices were improved for many producers and there has been an increase in exports by smallholders. However, the project found that changing agricultural practices and hygiene as well as increasing record-keeping by small farmers was difficult. The lack of skilled personnel to train compliance in private standards as well as lack of basic infrastructures in certain rural areas also contributed to limit smallholder upgrading. The market fundamentals also changed over the project period, with the entry of new players and increased competition in markets. Thus project findings recommend that future efforts reflect carefully on the time needed to induce fundamental changes and that those initiatives be closely aligned with market developments. Given the time needed to upgrade production standards for smallholders it is important to begin the process as rapidly as possible. Myanmar could greatly benefit from participating in the World Bank Global Food Safety Partnership which would provide additional resources and capacity to improve its food safety compliance.

Source: World Bank (2014), *Global Food Chain Partnerships*, World Bank, Washington DC, *www.worldbank.org/en/topic/agriculture/brief/global-food-safety-partnership*.

Build the Myanmar brand

The government could also proactively support the creation of the Myanmar agricultural brand. A communication strategy could include participating in trade fairs and liaison with foreign trade offices, as well as establishing a website to promote Myanmar's products. For example, in the rice sector, markets are moving to quality-defined branded products. Branding of specific high quality rice varieties, such as Pawsan, could therefore be envisaged. Chile's ProChile export promotion agency is a good example of how government support can support brand-building and exports (Box 2.2).

Box 2.2. **ProChile: Promoting Chilean products abroad**

ProChile, the trade promotion division of the Ministry for Foreign Affairs, was created in 1974 to gather market information and promote Chilean products abroad. ProChile's promotion activities are considered to have had a significant effect on Chile's exports of food and wine.

ProChile provides support to small and medium-sized enterprises so that they can access international markets. ProChile has a world-wide network, with trade offices and agencies located in over 35 countries, covering 90% of Chile's export markets. The offices are run by specialised teams that use their market expertise to help Chilean export companies conduct their international operations. ProChile also possesses 12 domestic regional offices which foster the development of goods and services suitable for export throughout the entire national territory. These offices – along with regional governments, the private sector, universities and other organisations – work together to identify the range of regional products and services for export and to develop appropriate trade promotion plans (ProChile, 2007).

Source: OECD (2008), *OECD Review of Agricultural Policies: Chile 2008*, http://dx.doi.org/10.1787/9789264042247-en.

Build and improve the infrastructure necessary to value chains, and improve industrial/economic zone policies

Existing industrial/economic zones lack the infrastructure necessary to meet international standards (e.g. electricity supply, transportation, waste water management, worker safety standards, cold storage facilities...) on which value chains and a vibrant export sector depends. The government is developing a nationwide strategic plan on industrial and economic zones with a view to facilitate exports. A nationwide plan should consider each zone's strategic location and objectives, and the general focus on value chains and exports. This would ensure that the zones complement Myanmar's development strategy by both reducing the costs along the value chain and overcoming some infrastructure constraints.

To be realised, these plans needed to be matched by an increase in investment for infrastructure more generally, and particularly in the transport and logistic sectors. This could include upgrading and expanding road networks, and improving the skills and training of workers in the sectors. The transport and logistic sectors' development has likely been hampered by the government-supported, below-cost pricing by state-owned enterprises (SOEs). Liberalising the sector could help spur investment. Streamlining responsibilities for transport and logistics between government agencies could also support the sector's development. For instance, overlapping responsibilities between the Ministry for Transport, Ministry for Rail Transport and the Ministry of Construction should be identified and streamlined. Harmonising transport and logistic regulations with those of Myanmar's neighbours (e.g. per axle weight restrictions) could be another goal that would facilitate the development of cross-border transportation industries.

Help improve existing value chains and facilitate the building of new chains

Alternative organisational structures – for example, clusters and contracting – may provide greater impetus to modernisation

Clustering of value chains in a given area can allow firms to exploit synergies and linkages both vertically, between one stage and another, and horizontally among players at the same stage. Clustering in agriculture has been found to improve the competitiveness of firms/farms due to benefits from collaboration as well as economies of scale in the provision of services and government support. This proximity of firms and farms at different stages of the value chain can create firm/farm linkages that initiate dialogue and collaboration to resolve common problems affecting the entire chain, such as implementation of standards or improvement of market information and access (Galvez-Nogales, 2010). However, catalysing such collaboration and interaction most often requires support of local government institutions and professional associations. These provide help in meeting objectives through technical assistance, training programmes and market research as well as professional support for its strategic development. Their participation is considered fundamental to the take-off and development of clusters. Stimulating the development inclusive value chains, particularly for high-value products such as fruits and vegetables, often requires striking a fragile balance promoting smallholder inclusion and economic viability of commercial operations.

With Myanmar's large potential in fruit and vegetable production, the cluster approach may be more beneficial to promoting growth and meeting standards than the present unorganised approach, particularly if smallholders are to be included. It could also make better use of plant packaging facilities and promote collaborative efforts to finance storage and treatment facilities necessary for market entry. These benefits could also be realised without a formal cluster as in the case of Myanmar's fish-processing industry, which shares processing plants. However, the structure and membership of the cluster might facilitate such activities more rapidly by fostering associative actions. Kenya's experience with smallholders provides some insights into this approach that might be adapted to Myanmar (Box 2.3).

Contract farming remains the general approach to incorporate small farmers into markets where it is important to ensure quality, safety and delivery volumes for buyers. In Viet Nam, over 90% of cotton and fresh milk and over 40% of tea and rice production are done through contract farming, and in China some 18 billion hectares were planted under contract farming arrangements in 2001 (Guo et al., 2005; Prowse, 2012; Hue, 2004). Contracting is widely used in India for seed, poultry, dairy, potatoes, rice and horticulture.

Contracts provide for acquisition of inputs through credit, for technical assistance and for a guaranteed price at harvest, thus relaxing the constraints the typical farmer faces in these areas. Research has found that the use of contracts tends to increase incomes of smallholders compared to those farmers not using contracts (Miyata et al., 2009; Da Silva, 2009; Prowse, 2012). Given that Myanmar's small farmers are constrained by a lack of quality inputs, credit and technical assistance, the use of contract farming to integrate farmers into value chains could be an economically viable solution for farmers and exporters as well as agri-food processors aiming to expand markets. From a public policy perspective, there is a role for government to support the establishment of contract farming where smallholders are involved.

Box 2.3. **Kenya's avocado cluster: How it was done**

Kenya's experience in building an avocado cluster may be instructive in understanding how clusters could improve output, inclusiveness and linkages to non-agricultural activities, although caution is needed in transferring experiences across countries.

The cluster project organised Kenya's small, resource-poor farmers into producer groups that were able to access inputs, improved quality control and linkages to diversified markets including higher-priced export markets and the lower-priced processing sector market. The cluster project also created non-agricultural firms and employment to service the agricultural sector and its downstream activities, such as transport, processing and marketing. While the initial conditions of avocado farmers in Kenya resembled those of many present producers in Myanmar, they operated in a business and institutional environment with substantial experience in exporting to high-value markets and in developing new products for markets that are only applicable to avocados. Myanmar's market position is significantly different in that it lacks basic infrastructures, support institutions and a business community with substantial experience in meeting evolving market demands.

Though the approach cannot be applied in its entirety, different aspects of the Kenya example could prove beneficial in Myanmar. These include the building of producer-trader associations and the involvement of local government and health authorities in defining strategies to improve food safety, efficiency and competitiveness in the different sectors.

Source: Jones and Webber (2010), "Achieving synergies through clustering – Kenyan avocados"; C.W. Webber and P. Labaste (eds.), *Building Competitiveness in Africa's Agriculture: A Guide to Value Chains Concepts and Applications*, World Bank, Washington, DC.

There are opportunities for contract farming in the fruit and vegetables sector, where quality and safety requirements need to be ensured all along the chain. Given Myanmar's potential for production of these crops, contract farming may provide a useful way to increase inclusiveness of very small farmers, since even one hectare of production can be highly remunerative. Incentives for contract production and value chain activities could be provided through tax concessions or access to preferential loans. Ensuring a transparent legal framework for contracts between farmers and agribusiness needs to be considered as the sectors develop.

Streamline the regulatory regime for manufacturers

To support manufacturing, the regulatory regime for manufacturers could be made more efficient and transparent. One-stop service centres to handle the compliance needs of businesses (e.g. registration, licensing and tax collections) are a good way of improving efficiency. One such service centre now exists in Yangon. Established by the Directorate of Investment and Company Administration (DICA), the centre is tasked with issuing company registration cards, export and import licences and renewing visas within one day, co-ordinating the work of eight relevant ministries. Other measures to improve the regulatory regime could include creating an SME development agency to perform cost-benefit analyses of regulations, and establishing a clear policy for procurements. Regular surveys of and consultation with manufacturers, business associations and investors should complement the more general industrial zone surveys currently in place, and better inform the government's action plans.

The government could also consider providing temporary tax breaks and/or access to finance to under-developed parts of value chains. These measures could be introduced along with sunset clauses and clearly defined criteria or date for when the measure would be withdrawn.

Research and rural training for the 21st century

Part of the constraint on structural transformation stems from low agricultural productivity due to inadequate agronomic skills and knowledge, limited extension services, an inefficient top-down approach to technological transfer, and the low overall level of education and vocational training in Myanmar. There is also a related lack of research and development (R&D) on improving production techniques and product quality. Indeed, the policy dialogue confirmed the need for a low-cost and efficient education programme for farmers and rural businesses. Skill shortages and mismatches in manufacturing and services, partly due to a supply- rather than demand-driven vocational curricula, similarly constrain other parts of the value chain. The following recommendations encompass this aspect as well as a more general strategy for raising the overall education level.

Dedicate more resources to research, including on high-value crops

One of the most effective ways for the government to increase incomes in agriculture is through expenditure on R&D with the aim to increase agricultural productivity and to promote innovation in products and processes. R&D is fundamental for adapting products to meet different quality standards under different agro-ecological conditions.

Investment in agricultural R&D in Myanmar is fairly low but has been increasing. For example, the capital budgets for the Department of Agricultural Research (DAR) and Yezin Agricultural University, its main agricultural research university, increased from 0.004% of the Ministry of Agriculture and Irrigation's budget in 2013/14 to over 4% in 2014/15, showing an important move in the right direction.

Limited funding for R&D for varieties adapted to local conditions has meant that production and distribution of high quality seeds has not been able to keep up with the needs of the agriculture sector. Furthermore, research has focused on rice and, more recently, pulses, but has essentially neglected the possibilities offered by other high-value crops and plants.

Disseminate information to farmers and rural businesses more efficiently

Establish rural training hubs

To raise incomes in rural areas, increasing the productivity of the agricultural sector is fundamental, but so too is providing an enabling environment for transitioning to value added products and developing a service sector. Providing appropriate education and training for rural communities can be an important part of this transformation. Currently government extension officers and managers of the Department of Agriculture cannot reach many farmers at the village level for several reasons, among them a lack of resources. The suggestion is therefore to create rural training hubs that provide education and training for Myanmar's 2 million smallholder commercial farmers (defined here as farms between 2 and 20 hectares) as well as agro-food entrepreneurs and SMEs, through both formal and informal (peer to peer) training.

The rural training hubs would serve as a meeting place for the different actors involved in agri-food chains. While the farmer training provided in the hubs would target smallholder commercial farmers, the information and training for small businesses in agriculture-related industries (such as processing, packaging, sorting...) could help stimulate off-farm employment, including for landless people or subsistence farmers[1] who struggle to generate profit from their small plots of land. In this way, the rural training hubs would serve more than the strictly farming community, representing an integrated approach to rural development.

Information delivered through the hubs could come from a range of sources. Exporters could take the role of trainers in the rural training hubs, as they have knowledge about market requirements, especially international markets. Equally, the hubs could be the vehicle for delivering technical assistance from development partners, enabling farmers and local businesses to tap into the wealth of existing knowledge. The precise courses taught would need to be adapted to the local needs (e.g. agricultural education focusing on special crops for delta, dry zone and hilly areas). It would also be essential that trainers are able to effectively communicate knowledge and information to farmers and rural communities.

Strengthen linkages and information flows between institutions involved in agricultural research and education

Stronger linkages between the Department of Agriculture (DOA), Department of Agricultural Research (DAR), state agricultural institutes, educational institutions (including agricultural universities and vocational institutions), and between farmers and these institutions would mean that farmers could receive information on new varieties and technologies and also that research carried out in these institutions could respond to farmers' needs.

Yezin Agricultural University (YAU), State Agricultural Institutes and TVET schools could link up with DOA officials who are currently working at the township and regional levels. DOA extension officers and managers could become extension education and advisory service providers, expanding their current role of collecting data from farmers on yields etc. In collaboration with township agricultural research farms and seed farms, DOA officials working in rural training hubs could disseminate information on new varieties and technologies. Part of their role would also be to listen to farmers' needs, challenges and problems; provide information if they can already suggest a solution; or if they cannot, to transmit these problems back to specialists and experts (e.g. at YAU, DOA, DAR) who can undertake research to find solutions.

Another way of ensuring that extension services are meeting farmers' needs is by charging fees for courses for commercial smallholders. Willingness to pay reveals the needs of farmers: if they are not willing to pay for the information, it is a signal that they may have other sources for this information or not think that it is worth it. This is crucial to avoid financing unnecessary extension information. For small, very poor subsistence farmers, paying even small fees for courses may be out of their reach and therefore counterproductive.

Use information and communication technology

Information and communication technology (ICT), including mobile phones, can be used to modernise agricultural extension education and advisory services, such as crop technology, weather, market information, etc. This has proved to be an effective, efficient and low-cost education model in many developing countries around the world (Box 2.4). Mobile phone ownership is growing in Myanmar's rural areas, opening up ICT as a viable solution to getting much-needed information to farmers.

Box 2.4. **ICT: Improving market price information dissemination**

Accessing up-to-date price information at different local market locations can improve farmers' decision making and incomes. Market information services using mobile technologies can provide tailored access to up-to-date local market information. These are generally offered by the private sector and are often fee-based unless subsidised by public authorities. Examples include:

India: *Reuters Market Light (RML)* fee-based mobile phone dissemination of price and market data. It now has 1.3 million subscribers and provides information in eight languages for over 300 crops. *www.reutersmarketlight.com*

Thailand: *1677 Farmer Information Superhighway* mobile phone dissemination of essential agricultural market information for free. There are now 250 000 subscribers and over 40 business and state agencies collaborate in the programme's material development. A competition to improve applications is held each year. *www.telenor.com/sustainability/initiatives-worldwide/using-mobile-to-improve-farming-skills/*

Pakistan and Bangladesh: Mobile phone dissemination of price and markets information, with daily SMS alerts. It allows farmers to calculate where to get the best price using the app of the Agricultural Commodity Trade project. *www.telenor.com/sustainability/initiatives-worldwide/pakistan/*

Senegal and Ghana: *Manobi and Esoko* mobile phone dissemination of market information in collaboration with government, business and international organisations. Both operate in a number of countries in Africa. *www.manobi.sn* and *www.esoko.com*

Traditional ICT tools such as radio are still widely used to disseminate price information on a daily or more frequent basis particularly where phone or Internet access is unavailable or where literacy and costs are too constraining. The content varies widely: some provide only national or regional data while community-based radio stations provide local market information. For instance in Mozambique, community radio programmes disseminate local market prices, transportation costs and quantities. *www.farmradio.org*

Scale up provision of quality technical and vocational education and training

While farmer education and effective extension services can help raise agricultural productivity, other parts of the agricultural value chain – the manufacturing and services that transform and move a product from the agricultural producer to the consumer – likewise need workers with the right skills. In Myanmar, skill shortages and mismatches in manufacturing and services, partly due to a supply- rather than demand-driven vocational curricula, constrain parts of the value chain. Firms in Myanmar identify a lack of skilled workers as a serious or very serious obstacle to their operations and one that ranks ahead of any other obstacle (OECD, UMFCCI and UNESCAP, 2014).

Adjust the current basic education system from one geared towards preparing a limited number of students for university to one that also allows for technical and vocational training as end-goals.

The basic education system – including its curriculum, structure and the final matriculation exam – is geared towards preparing students for university, a goal few ever reach. More options for technical and vocational education (TVET) would better serve the needs of an industrialising economy such as that of Myanmar and would provide more useful skills to the large numbers of students who do not reach higher education. The proportion of students enrolled in technical and vocational education at the upper secondary level was just 0.5% in the 2013-14 academic year, which is very low compared to other countries in the region (Figure 2.3).

Figure 2.3. **Secondary technical and vocational education and training (TVET) is extremely limited in Myanmar**

Technical/vocational enrolment at the upper secondary level as % of total enrolment in upper secondary

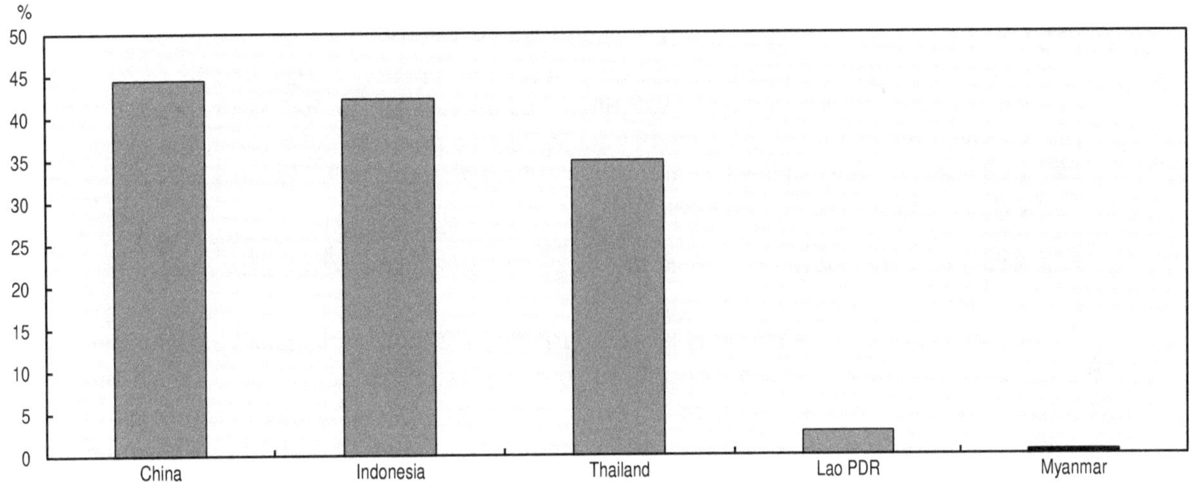

Note: Upper secondary education corresponds to the final stage of secondary education. Data are for 2012 except for Myanmar (academic year 2013-14) and Indonesia (2011).

Source: UNESCO (2014), *UNESCO Institute for Statistics Data Centre* (database), United Nations Educational, Scientific and Cultural Organization, *http://stats.uis.unesco.org/* and Ministry of Science and Technology, Union of Myanmar.

StatLink *http://dx.doi.org/10.1787/888933346863*

Efforts to increase provision may need to be matched with initiatives to improve the attractiveness of TVET as an option. In Myanmar, as in many countries, there is a negative perception of TVET and of manual work in general. Some countries are taking active measures to encourage students to enrol in TVET courses by improving the public perception of skills training. China, for example, provides opportunities for vocational secondary school students to be able to pursue higher education (tertiary level); since this policy there have been an increasing number of applicants for vocational schools (Ruth and Grollman, 2009). Other measures can also show that technical skills are valued. For example, China is setting up a national system of honours and rewards for "skills masters", and many countries take part in international skills competitions.

Align TVET courses and curricula with the needs of the labour market

To meet the needs of the labour market, TVET systems require strong and consistent engagement of employers, unions and the interests of students to ensure that the organisation and the content of programmes meet the needs of business and the wider economy. Myanmar could draw on examples of institutional arrangements used to involve social partners in other countries, such as Denmark's Advisory Council (Box 2.5). Designing courses to be practical rather than only theoretical, including workplace training, and ensuring that TVET teachers keep up-to-date with modern industry standards will also help ensure the relevance and quality of TVET.

Box 2.5. **Institutional frameworks to involve social partners in Denmark**

In *Denmark*, the Advisory Council for Initial Vocational Education and Training advises the Ministry of Education on all matters concerning the VET system (the Ministry of Education is the overall body responsible for the VET system in Denmark having responsibility for all legal, policy and programme definition aspects). For example, the Advisory Council is responsible for monitoring labour market trends and, on this basis, recommends the establishment of new qualifications. Its members represent the social partners, school leaders and teachers associations, and persons appointed by the Ministry of Education.

At the sectoral level employers and employees are equally represented in trade committees. They advise on specific VET qualifications relevant to their sector, ensure the relevance and quality of VET programmes in relation to the labour market, approve training places, and are responsible for the final VET examination (Journeyman's test) and for issuing certificates to VET trainees.

Source: Kuczera , et al. (2008),*OECD Reviews of Vocational Education and Training: A Learning for Jobs Review of Sweden 2008*, OECD Reviews of Vocational Education and Training, *http://dx.doi.org/10.1787/9789264113978-en*.

Once the systematic collection of labour market data is more established in Myanmar, this information could be used in addition to consultation to periodically revise the vocational training courses offered and their curricular to reflect changes in the demand for skills. Information could be gathered on education-to-work transitions through longitudinal surveys of individuals, and on the demand for skills through surveys, for example.

Facilitate skills upgrades and workplace training

Employers' organisations and government officials report that young people are often not "work ready" by the time they complete their initial education, or even after graduation from university. To tackle the challenge of skills mismatches, continued training for workers is essential.

Encourage investment in worker training

Employers currently invest very little in training their workforce. Over half of all firms do not spend anything on training for employees. Of the firms that did spend something on training, around 20% spent MMK 50 000-100 000 per employee per year (roughly USD 50-100) and another 20% spent MMK 10 000-500 000 per employee per year (roughly USD 100-500) (OECD, UMFCCI and UNESCAP, 2014).

However, the incentives for employers to invest in their employees may be insufficient, even if the employers benefit from such investments. For example, individual firms may be unwilling to provide training if their employees are likely to leave for a competitor, once trained. 41% of firms in Myanmar reporting skills problems with their workforce identified skilled employees moving to other firms as a particular challenge. The fishing sector and the hotels and restaurant sector most frequently reported problems with skilled employees leaving for other firms.

To allay employer concerns about transferrable skills and losing trained employees to competitors, the government could work with business associations to provide industry-specific training, funded by membership contributions, or even directly finance training programmes for sectors where employers are most reluctant to invest and for individuals with low skills. This could be funded by levying a small tax on businesses to finance training.

Modernising agricultural finance

The rural sector's lack of ready access to credit has constrained productivity and slowed structural transformation. Although this is due in part to the underdevelopment of Myanmar's financial system in general, the problem appears to be particularly acute in the rural sector. Of all the segments of the Myanmar economy, the rural sector is the most underserved by the formal financial system: only about 2.5% of total loans go to the rural sector, even though it accounts for 30% of GDP and two-thirds of employment. The Myanmar Agricultural Development Bank (MADB) has essentially been the only credit provider, and restrictions on loans mean they have been made mainly for rice crops. This has limited the ability for producers to upgrade (or even maintain) their production processes or to grow higher-value crops.

Participants in the policy dialogue unsurprisingly saw the reform of the MADB as a key measure. Yet reforming the MADB would not in itself resolve the underlying dynamics behind a lack of credit for certain sectors of the economy, nor could a single institution be capable of efficiently providing the full range of services needed by each sector. These could instead be addressed through the overall development of financial institutions and markets, which should expand the financial sector's coverage, increase the products and services on offer, and improve resource allocation. Finally, improving public finances is key to financing Myanmar's development plans and measures on both revenue and expenditure management are considered.

Expand financial services available to the rural economy

The rural economy requires a wide range of financial services, offered by a variety of institutions, if it is to develop (Table 2.1). No single type of financial institution is capable of efficiently providing the full range of financial products and services. Microfinance, for example, can help to meet the short-term needs of farmers and help to finance microbusinesses, but it is not so suitable for larger businesses, or for capital accumulation and innovation. Effective rural financial systems encompass a variety of institutions, including commercial banks, development finance institutions, microfinance institutions (MFIs), and specialised financial services such as leasing and finance companies.

Implement measures that expand farmers' access to formal financial services

Farmers' access to credit could be improved by providing incentives for commercial banks to operate in the agricultural sector, both to receive deposits and to distribute loans. Currently banks are hesitant to lend to the agricultural sector given perceived risks, including the impact of climate change (i.e. extreme weather events). Raising the ceiling on bank lending rates, which does not at present allow banks to recover the costs of lending to smaller and underserved segments, will be critical to improving access to credit and to giving banks the incentives to extend their reach into the rural economy. Farmers' access to credit should increase thanks to the newly-introduced Land Use Certificates, which are intended to be used by farmers as collateral for loans. Their use in the commercial banking system should be monitored either through bank reporting obligations or special surveys.

The microfinance sector should gradually broaden the range of products and services it offers as the industry matures and the experience level and skills of MFIs and the supervisory authorities increase. Consideration could be given to phasing in higher capital requirements for MFIs, especially those that take deposits. The supervisory responsibilities for MFIs may also need to be modified in certain areas. For example, the Central Bank of Myanmar needs to be involved in the oversight of deposit-taking MFIs and arrangements for co-ordinating supervision among the Microfinance Supervisory Enterprise (MSE), the co-operatives supervisors and the Central Bank may also need to be strengthened.

Table 2.1. **Financing needs for the rural economy**

Financing need and type of client, based on international experience	Types of financial services required	Situation in Myanmar	Suitable financial institutions or other providers based on international experience	In Myanmar
Purchase of inputs	Short-term working capital credit	Not sufficiently available in Myanmar at affordable interest rates	Rural banks, financial co-operatives, input providers financed by commercial banks, some MFIs	MADB, some commercial banks for larger loans to input suppliers, some MFIs having the capability to do rural lending, informal lenders
Post-harvest consumption needs (in order to avoid having to sell products right at harvest time)	Warehouse receipt financing, inventory credit	Difficult in Myanmar since there are few village-based storage opportunities, no legal framework for warehouse receipt financing	Commercial banks, specialised agricultural banks, some MFIs with special knowledge	Not available
Micro-entrepreneurs	Short-term credit, savings, money transfer	Informal credit at very high rates available, no savings or money transfer services	MFI, village-based savings and credit groups, financial co-operatives	MFIs provide some credit, no savings or money transfer services
SMEs	Working capital and investment credit, money transfer	No money transfer services and little investment credit available, credit lines available for traders and brokers	Commercial banks	Commercial banks
Purchase of agricultural equipment (some scale irrigation, tractors, etc.)	Medium-term credit	Available to any significant extent for movable equipment, not available for small-scale irrigation needs	Commercial banks and leasing companies, equipment dealers	Some commercial banks and equipment dealers
Purchase of food and other consumption needs	Savings in order to manage household budgets, credit only if there is the ability to repay, transfers from government or other services	Savings not available, informal lenders provide credit at very high costs, No government transfer services could be observed	MFIs, village-based savings and credit Institutions, financial co-operatives	Some MFIs, informal lenders
Savings gathering	Financial Institution deposits, including interest bearing for non-demand accounts	Limited by limited bank branch networks and lack of confidence in formal FIs	Commercial banks; deposit taking MFIs; credit co-operatives	MADB; some MFIs and co-operatives
Payments services	Demand deposits and money transfer services	Limited by limited bank branch networks; lack of confidence in formal financial institutions; limited payments infrastructure	Commercial banks; international payment companies; some MFIs and co-operatives	MADB; some MFIs and co-operatives
Insurance services	Crop insurance; casualty and health insurance	Limited by restricted scope of main insurer and lack of private insurers specialising in rural sector; Myanma Insurance provides snake-bite cover for farmers in rural areas; weather index-based crop insurance is not yet feasible due to underdeveloped network of weather stations.	Life and non-life insurance companies	Myanmar Insurance; new private insurers

Note: MADB = Myanmar Agricultural Development Bank; MFI = microfinance institutions.

Source: Adapted from Kloeppinger-Todd and Sandar (2013), "Rural finance in Myanmar", *Background Paper*, No. 3 prepared for the Strategic Agricultural Sector and Food Security Diagnostic for Myanmar, led by Michigan State University and in partnership with the Myanmar Development Resource Institute – Centre for Economic and Social Development (MDRI-CESD), January.

Other services, such as leasing, warehouse financing facilities and crop insurance could also support the development of the rural sector. The development of a leasing industry would help to boost productivity in the agricultural sector as well as the development of rural small enterprises by improving access to credit for machinery purchases. Public-private partnerships could be used to expand warehouse financing facilities to enable farmers to extend their loan repayment periods beyond harvest time, when prices are at their lowest. Finally, a weather index-based crop insurance scheme would help mitigate losses to farmers from catastrophic climate risks such as floods and droughts. Weather index-based schemes are applied to the entire farm community and are less complex to operate than traditional crop insurance schemes that require detailed farm-level data. In order for weather index-based crop insurance to be introduced in Myanmar however, the country's network of weather stations would need to be extended and upgraded as they are currently not dense enough. Crop insurance schemes will also require an insurance regulatory environment that permits the extension of insurance products to the rural sector and the development of new products suited to its distinctive needs. The regulatory environment must also provide oversight to ensure that activities are carried out in accordance with sound prudential principles.

Myanmar's Financial Inclusion Roadmap 2014-2020, overseen by an inter-ministerial steering committee chaired by the Deputy Minister of Finance, has been established to address the issue of financial inclusion.

Reform the Myanmar Agricultural Development Bank

Participants identified the reform of the Myanmar Agricultural Development Bank (MADB) – effectively the only credit provider for farmers at present – as an important way to improve financing for rural areas. The MADB's present network of branches across the country and local knowledge of credit needs/risks means that expansion of its financial services and development of its commercial banking capabilities could allow it to become an effective and vibrant rural financial institution. Successful transformations from state rural lending institutions to commercial rural banking systems include Bank Rakyat of Indonesia, the Agricultural Bank of Mongolia and the rural lending institutions of Thailand.

A functioning, reformed MADB could be one part of an effective rural financial system encompassing a variety of other institutions such as commercial banks, development finance institutions, microfinance providers and specialist services providers such as leasing companies.

The government should continue the corporatisation process for the MADB, with the aim of making a broader range of rural lending its focus. The establishment of MADB as a commercial entity will require the separation of the non-commercial policy functions from their commercial banking activities.

There are two options for dealing with the policy lending and other non-commercial functions (namely to make a variety of loans to the rural sector, not all of which might be commercially viable) now performed by MADB. The first is to remove these functions from the bank to allow it to focus exclusively on commercial banking and to transfer the functions to separate non-commercial development institutions or government departments. For example, the MADB might be divided into a commercial bank and a development bank, with the latter carrying out its subsidised lending with the loan subsidies provided, say, by the MOAI and financed by borrowing at market rates from other banks.

Alternatively, the central government could leave the subsidised lending and other policy functions with the state-controlled banks but compensate them for these services. Under this model, the MADB would continue to administer the loan programmes for farmers under criteria set by the government. This would require the government to provide explicit loan subsidies (from the budget) to the MADB equal to the difference between the commercial interest rate and subsidised rate, and to similarly pay the market cost plus a profit margin for currency and other policy services. This option involves less restructuring of existing institutions than the first but it could divert resources and focus from the bank's commercial activities. Overall, the experience in other countries, notably China, suggests that the first option is likely to be the more effective.

Participants in the policy dialogue event advocated for the division of MADB into a development bank and a commercial bank. They proposed that the development bank be transferred to the Ministry of Finance under the supervision of the Central Bank, and that it be tasked with funding subsidised loans to poor, smallholder farmers. Very low-interest rate Official Development Assistance (ODA) loans from development partners were suggested as a potential additional source of funding for this bank.

Participants suggested a number of measures regarding the commercial entity of this reformed MADB. First, its lending rate should be increased to the commercial rate (currently 13.8%). Second, it could offer other services, such as leasing and warehouse financing. Finally, if this approach were adopted, participants proposed amending the law governing MADB's profit-sharing, which currently sees 75% of the net profit of MADB channelled to the government budget, something participants saw as jeopardising the sustainability of the bank.

To be effective as a commercial entity, the MADB will need to have management autonomy in its business decisions, including its lending, even if the state continues to have a controlling interest in its ownership. Actions also need to be taken to improve the governance, transparency and accountability of the MADB. This would include legislative change regarding corporatisation, reforms to the management structure, and improvements to information management and disclosure. Participants stressed the need to maintain certain strengths of the MADB, such as the low rate of non-performing loans.

Effective risk management, for MADB but equally for the whole banking sector, emerged as a preoccupation for participants. Risks linked to climate change (e.g. floods, drought) but also political, inflation, and exchange rate risks were cited as particular concerns.

Develop formal financial institutions and markets

Changes to the rural finance system would need to be part of broader financial market reform, shifting away from a command approach to one that provides appropriate incentives for financial institutions to innovate and operate sustainably in the market without threatening systemic stability. This would include eliminating the ceiling on bank lending and deposit rates (and allowing these to move with market rates once the relevant markets have been established) and relaxing the requirement that all lending must be secured. Moreover, restrictions on foreign bank entry should be relaxed since they have more capacity to provide sophisticated financial services, keeping in mind that the terms under which these banks are allowed to enter could affect the products they are willing to offer.

Resolve any conflict of interest between the commercial and regulatory objectives of government interests in the sector

At present there are some conflicts of interest between the commercial and regulatory objectives of government interests, e.g. commercial operations taken by the insurance regulator. As noted above, one way to separate policy functions from commercial activities would be to transfer all policy functions to government departments or non-commercial development institutions (e.g. transferring the currency functions of the Myanma Economic Bank to the central bank or to the Ministry of Finance). In the longer term, all state-owned banks should be reformed into commercial entities (Box 2.6).

Box 2.6. **Best practice for the commercialisation of state-owned enterprises**

The OECD Guidelines on Corporate Governance of State-Owned Enterprises (SOEs) are recommendations to governments on how to ensure that SOEs operate efficiently, transparently and in an accountable manner, and can provide a "blueprint" for the corporatisation and commercialisation of SOEs.

The commercialisation of Myanmar's state-owned banks would entail their transformation into profit-making commercial ventures without subsidies from the state. In cases where the banks combine economic activities with public policy functions, high standards of transparency and disclosure regarding the cost of public policy functions and revenue structures must be maintained, allowing for an attribution to main activity areas. The Guidelines recommend that costs related to achieving public policy objectives should be funded by the state and disclosed.

The Guidelines provide seven overarching recommendations to professionalise the state as an owner and ensure that competition between SOEs and private enterprises is conducted on a level playing field.

1. ***Rationales for state ownership:*** The state exercises the ownership of SOEs in the interest of the general public. It should carefully evaluate and disclose the objectives that justify state ownership and subject these to a recurrent review.
2. ***The state's role as an owner:*** The state should act as an informed and active owner, ensuring that the governance of SOEs is carried out in a transparent and accountable manner, with a high degree of professionalism and effectiveness,

   e.g. the government should allow SOEs full operational autonomy to achieve their defined objectives and refrain from intervening in management.
3. ***State-owned enterprises in the marketplace:*** Consistent with the rationale for state ownership, the legal and regulatory framework for SOEs should ensure a level playing field and fair competition in the marketplace when SOEs undertake economic activities,

   e.g. clear separation between the state's ownership function and other state functions that may influence the conditions for SOEs (e.g. market regulation); SOEs should not be exempt from general laws, tax codes and regulations; SOEs' economic activities should not benefit from any indirect financial support that confers an advantage over private competitors, and their economic activities should not receive inputs (such as energy, water or land) at prices or conditions more favourable than those available to private competitors.
4. ***Equitable treatment of shareholders and other investors:*** Where SOEs are listed or otherwise include non-state investors among their owners, the state and the enterprises should recognise the rights of all shareholders and ensure shareholders' equitable treatment and equal access to corporate information.
5. ***Stakeholder relations and responsible business:*** The state ownership policy should fully recognise SOEs' responsibilities towards stakeholders and request that SOEs report on their relations with stakeholders. It should make clear any expectations the state has in respect of responsible business conduct by SOEs.

Box 2.6. **Best practice for the commercialisation of state-owned enterprises** *(cont.)*

6. Disclosure and transparency: State-owned enterprises should observe high standards of transparency and be subject to the same high quality accounting, disclosure, compliance and auditing standards as listed companies.

7. The responsibilities of the boards of state-owned enterprises: The boards of SOEs should have the necessary authority, competencies and objectivity to carry out their functions of strategic guidance and monitoring of management. They should act with integrity and be held accountable for their actions.

Examples of corporatised state-owned banks in other countries may provide useful lessons for Myanmar.

Bank Rakyat Indonesia

The Bank Rakyat of Indonesia underwent two major periods of reform, first of its micro-banking units in 1984 following the economic crisis in 1982 and another organisation-wide reform following the 1997-98 Asian financial crisis. The reforms have been credited with transforming BRI from a loss-making state-owned bank into a highly profitable organisation with a large micro-banking network. A review of BRI's reform concluded the following key features for success (Seibel and Ozaki, 2009):

- An independent board of directors free of government interference as well as a code of conduct.
- Positive changes in corporate culture and mindset that encourages communication and transparency and includes performance targets and incentives, and risk and compliance management.
- A strategy to expand outreach in order to improve inclusiveness: BRI expanded its outreach to other segments of the population (i.e. not only farmers, crop agriculture, and seasonal loans, but to any creditworthy person for any income-generating activity) and diversified products (e.g. savings, not only credit).
- BRI's organisational reforms were also successful thanks to broader financial sector liberalisation in parallel with appropriate supervision and prudential regulation (e.g. effective internal controls, "fit and proper" tests for senior management...)

The Development Bank of South Africa

The Development Bank of South Africa (DBSA) is one of four state-owned development banks in the country, operating primarily in the infrastructure sector in South Africa but also in neighbouring countries. The bank has both commercial and social objectives. DBSA's taxable profits from its commercial operations are channelled to a subsidiary body – the DBSA Development Fund – whose main objective is to provide support to low-income municipalities through grants, technical expertise and training (Beck et al, 2011). DBSA's success has been attributed to its good corporate governance structure, including: an independent and qualified board of directors; professional management; and the South African Treasury as an active shareholder (Rudolph, 2009).

Sources: Beck, Munzele Maimbo, Faye and Triki (2011), *Financing Africa: Through the crisis and beyond*, International Bank for Reconstruction and Development/World Bank, Washington, DC; OECD (2015b), *OECD Guidelines on Corporate Governance of State-Owned Enterprises*, 2015 Edition, *http://dx.doi.org/10.1787/9789264244160-en*; Rudolph (2009), "State Financial Institutions: Mandates, Governance, and Beyond", *Policy Research Working Paper* 5141, World Bank, Washington, DC; Seibeland Ozaki (2009), "Restructuring of state-owned financial institutions: Lessons from Bank Rakyat Indonesia", Asian Development Bank, Mandaluyong City.

Implement an appropriate regulatory and supervisory framework to support these developments

An effective financial system requires the appropriate regulatory and supervisory framework. For instance, supervisory responsibilities could be streamlined, unduly stringent restrictions (e.g. collateral criteria that bear little relation to the credit risks posed) should be relaxed, and the framework should help institutions develop appropriate risk assessment criteria for their lending decisions (e.g. through capital requirements and loan-to-value restrictions). The regulatory regime on microfinance institutions should also be clarified, and consideration given to phasing in higher capital requirements to levels commensurate with those applying to microfinance institutions in other countries in the region.

Facilitate the development of securities and credit markets

Securities and credit markets could be developed by first focusing on the infrastructure, regulatory capabilities and other factors (e.g. links to the ASEAN region for equities markets) that are necessary for such markets. Once these are in place, the development of a domestic interbank market should be a priority, followed by the secondary government bond market: the former would enable rural financial institutions to be integrated into the financial system, and both markets would help establish market-based interest rates.

Strengthen public financial management and revenue collection

Facilitate investment by improving the regulatory framework on aid funding and foreign investment

External sources could provide as much as one-quarter to one-third of Myanmar's financing needs for development through at least the remainder of this decade.

Improved regulatory frameworks and processes should facilitate more foreign investment. Strategies could include making legislative clauses on investor protection more specific, reducing the discretion of the Myanmar Investment Commission (MIC) in the approval process, and improving the "soft" infrastructure to make it easier to start a business and for businesses to enforce contracts. Provisions for investor protection are included in the Myanmar Investment Law that is currently being drafted. Also, since the MDCR review was published, MIC's authority on investment has been transferred to regional and state governments through amendments to the Foreign Investment Law and the Myanmar Citizens Investment Law. The OECD Investment Policy Review of Myanmar (2014a) provides comprehensive recommendations to encourage and facilitate investment, both domestic and foreign.

Given the expected increases in ODA to Myanmar, it will be advisable to streamline and revise the approval procedures for ODA funding. Recommendations include setting a threshold to exempt smaller projects from the formal approval process. Procedures could also be streamlined by combining the Foreign Aid Management Central Committee with the Foreign Aid Management Working Committee.

Improve public finances through structural tax reforms, improved collection and administration

Although levels are increasing, ODA and FDI flows are unlikely to be sustained at such a level indefinitely. As development proceeds and the most productive foreign investments are exhausted, the flows are likely to recede. The bulk of the financial resources to support development will come from government revenues and domestic savings.

Both government revenues and domestic savings have been depressed by excessive regulation and other legacies of the pre-reform system and will need to rise substantially. Government revenues, especially tax revenues, are exceptionally low compared to other Asian developing countries. Gross national savings (GDP less final consumption expenditure) have risen significantly since 2010, to an estimated rate of about 24.5% of GDP in 2012 from 15.8% in 2009, but are still short of the levels of 30% or more attained by Viet Nam and most other rapidly growing ASEAN economies (United Nations, 2013).

Myanmar could reduce the reliance on direct taxes, and consider raising the tax rate to be closer to that of Myanmar's ASEAN neighbours (e.g. 7-10%) once the value-added tax has replaced the commercial tax. Furthermore, it will be important to establish a comprehensive set of regulations for tax administration. This should address in part the currently very limited and fragmented taxpayer registration, where only 0.4% of the population are registered taxpayers. To improve tax collection, Myanmar could move to a self-assessment system rather than a partial audit of every taxpayer, and re-organise collection to be based on taxpayer types (e.g. large taxpayers) rather than tax type.

A number of these recommendations are included in Myanmar's comprehensive long-term plan, in place since April 2015. For example, large taxpayer and medium taxpayer offices have been established and a self-assessment system has been introduced in the large taxpayer office, with plans to introduce this system into the medium taxpayer office. A new value-added tax law is due to begin in the 2018 fiscal year.

Strengthen public financial management

Increasing tax revenues needs to be accompanied by an ongoing evolutionary process of public financial management (PFM) reform to improve government capabilities to ensure that revenues are allocated in line with development and other priorities, that public services are delivered efficiently, and that fiscal soundness and stability are maintained.

Myanmar's government has begun an extensive programme of PFM reforms to improve the effectiveness with which expenditures are allocated, financed and managed. The reforms taken so far have already yielded some significant accomplishments, especially in making the budget process more transparent to the public and more accountable to its elected representatives. A fiscal transparency team within the Ministry of Finance was also established in December 2015 to enhance public disclosure and public access to fiscal information. The team aims to increase the production and release of fiscal reports in the 2016-17 budget cycle compared to the previous cycle, and support the overall PFM efforts to improve the quality of fiscal information and analysis within the government, including links between budget programmes and national priorities.

Additional steps that could be taken include:

- Reporting the revenues from natural resources in a transparent manner.
- Making the Internal Revenue Department semi-autonomous under the Ministry of Finance.
- Allowing the Public Accounts Committee enough resources to prepare independent budget analyses.
- Improving the information provided (e.g. including forecasts) to the parliament in the budgetary process.

Better align the budgetary process with national development objectives

Improvement in the means by which development resources are allocated is as important as raising them from external and domestic sources. Ways to better align the budgetary process with national development objectives include:

- Using a medium-term fiscal framework instead of a year-to-year one.
- Significantly strengthening the linkage between the current and capital budgets with the objective to integrate current and capital budget formulation in the lead budget agency, following international best practice.

- Decreasing fiscal centralisation by increasing responsibilities at the local government level (e.g. for education and health) and setting clear criteria for revenue sharing and allocation transfers from the federal to the state/regional level.

Strengthening land rights

A strategy to improve land security would raise agricultural productivity, better align production with market demand, as well as improve the rural sector's access to finance. Any strategy should be aimed at removing uncertainty on land rights, which currently impedes efficient resource allocation and dampens incentives to produce and invest. In particular, participants saw the need for an overarching "mother law" on land to overcome contradictory laws and overlapping responsibility for the laws by different ministries. The decentralisation of land management was also identified as a priority.

Strengthen and clarify land rights, and improve production incentives by easing restrictions on land use

Resolve any conflict and ambiguity in the regulatory framework for land tenure and crop choice

State ownership of land and the underdeveloped rule of law have left land rights unclear in many cases. For example, the terms of land rights defined in the Farm Land Law and the Foreign Investment Law are not consistent. Some laws currently guarantee crop choice (e.g. *Protecting Rights and Enhancing Economic Welfare of Farmers Law* [2013]), while other laws require permission to change land-use designations. This has reduced incentives for investing in improving farmland and has limited farmers' abilities to use their properties to secure financing.

Consider any indirect restrictions on land use

This might include limits on loans for high-value crops, both in terms of the loan amount and the number of acres devoted to the crop. Restrictions (if any) should be decided only after studying market demand – particularly for export – by crop type and the cost of crop cultivation among other factors.

Complete the issuance of land use certificates to farmers to overcome the current lack of formal and centralised documentation on land ownership, and help farmers understand their purpose.

The Farmland Law, passed in 2012, attempts to address the challenge of land registration by creating official land use certificates (LUCs) clarifying famers' land rights. According to the Ministry of Agriculture and Irrigation, LUCs had been issued to over 98% of agricultural land holders by the end of 2015.

However, the availability of LUCs is not sufficient to ensure that these provide appropriate investment and production incentives to farmers given their lack of knowledge in how these might be employed to finance investment or production. The development of educational programmes on how to effectively use LUCs to finance investment and production are warranted to assist farmers in understanding the options these provide. Ongoing reforms that allow the LUCs to be used as collateral for loans could also be complemented by monitoring their acceptance as collateral by lenders.

Improve the administration of land laws

A coherent legal framework needs to be accompanied by improved government capacity to administer land laws. The Government of Myanmar could consider decentralising land management and clearly defining responsibilities at the central, regional, district and township levels. A first step could be an administrative council that oversees the decentralised structure, provides management support to local levels, and has the power to resolve land issues at all levels.

From expectation to action – moving towards participatory policy design

To be successful in the long run, any national development plan must be underpinned by a national consensus. The policy dialogue emphasised the need for any future vision for Myanmar to reflect citizens' needs and wants. To that end, participants suggested a strategy to collect more information through both new surveys and a review of existing surveys, and regular dialogue between citizens and policy makers. However, it would be just as important to remove obstacles to this process, including a weak capacity to implement policy, and distrust in the government or in the process of translating citizens' wishes into a coherent policy able to be implemented. A strategy could include the following general recommendations.

Improve civic participation in policy-making processes

The following recommendations are taken from the OECD Open Government Review of Myanmar (2014) that assessed the status of civic participation in Myanmar and suggested that the government of Myanmar combine different citizen participation tools.

Since 2011, the government has made efforts to engage the public in policy making, for example, by publishing draft laws for commentary, conducting open discussions with the public on legislation, and engaging in capacity-building workshops alongside civil society organisations. For example, the Association Registration Law was drafted with consultation from civil society organisations. These efforts, however, are ad-hoc, as not every piece of legislation has been open to public consultation, and the process for seeking public consultation is not mandated by any legislation or systematic process.

Myanmar could strengthen mechanisms to involve citizens in the policy-making process. Civic participation would benefit from making the consultation process systematic, consistent and transparent. It is widely accepted that to reach a diverse group of citizens and stakeholders, taking into account their diverging capabilities and access to government, different citizen participation tools should be combined (Box 2.7). Online consultation tools should for example be complemented by in-person consultation (OECD, 2014b).

Focusing on the subject of economic modernisation starting with agriculture, participants in the policy dialogue suggested organising public fora for dialogue between policy makers, farmers and other stakeholders. They also suggested reviewing existing polls, surveys that have been carried out on public expectations and preferences, and launching new polls to ensure that citizens are regularly consulted.

Strengthening capacity for implementation

The success of any national development vision and strategy rests on the public sector's capacity to implement policies. As the previous chapter showed, institutional capacity in

Myanmar is relatively weak, and resources to design and implement policies, both in terms of financing and expertise, are strained. Strengthening the public sector's capacity to design and implement policy will be as vital as ensuring that policy-making processes are participatory.

Box 2.7. **Consultation tools for policy making**

Using one consultation method alone may not be sufficient to reach out to stakeholders. A combination of a range of methods and a flexible approach helps to maximise the effectiveness of consultation. For example, a multi-channel approach can combine focus groups, institutional advisory boards, meetings organised in the regions and open consultation over the Internet, as illustrated in the following example.

The "Grenelle" forums in France

The Grenelle Environment Forum brought together the central government and representatives of civil society in order to draw up a road map for ecology, and sustainable development and planning, leading to the bill on environmental programming. The aim was to establish an action plan of 15-20 concrete and quantifiable measures that would meet with the broadest possible agreement among participants.

The Grenelle Environment Forum combined several forms of consultation, joint action and appeals for contributions, as part of a co-ordinated process:

- The first phase, from mid-July to the end of September 2007, was dedicated to dialogue and the preparation of proposals within 6 working groups consisting of 40 members drawn from 5 "colleges": the central government, local authorities, NGOs, employers and wage earners. They were given the task of identifying concerns and devising operational proposals to respond to them. These proposals were recorded in a set of reports.
- The second stage of the Grenelle Forum, from the end of September to mid-October 2007, was devoted to consultation with the public on the action proposals from the working groups, via different channels:
  - The government took stock of the opinions of various advisory boards, institutions or bodies, including Parliament: 31 councils and committees were consulted, and Parliament debated the proposals on 3 October in the National Assembly and on 4 October in the Senate.
  - Regional meetings were organised from 5-22 October 2007. Any citizen could take part by applying to the prefecture of the Department concerned. The government selected 17 towns (or cities) to host the meetings. These gatherings were often preceded by workshops chaired by prominent local people, which allowed first discussions of the proposals and presented conclusions of the national working groups. These regional meetings were attended by almost 17 000 participants in all, including elected representatives, people representing the economic, social and voluntary sectors, and ordinary citizens.
  - Finally, participation over the Internet was proposed: citizens were able to go online to comment on and suggest amendments to the proposals of the working groups on a website forum, from 28 September to 14 October. This method of online consultation was an unqualified success, with 72 000 visits and over 11 000 contributions published in 17 days.
- The third stage, on 24-26 October, resulted in negotiations and decisions. Within 4 panel discussions involving the 5 colleges, 268 commitments were identified.
- In the fourth stage (December 2007), 33 operational assignments were initiated to obtain proposals for action enabling the conclusions of the Grenelle Forum to be implemented.

The results of these assignments fed into the bill for environmental programming, which was passed by Parliament in June 2009. The act known as the Loi Grenelle 1 was followed by Grenelle 2. The two bills arising from Grenelle were the subject of an economic, social and environmental impact assessment, and were publicised on the Internet as soon as they were submitted to Parliament.

Source: OECD (2012a), *Regulatory Consultation: A MENA-OECD Practitioners' Guide for engaging Stakeholders in the rule-making process.*

Simplifying and streamlining the current policy-making frameworks could be a first step to easing the capacity constraint. Policy-making frameworks are often complex. For example, in the areas of education and vocational training, a total of 18 line ministries provide some technical or vocational training, and responsibility for higher education is divided between 13 ministries. This poses a challenge for the design and implementation of coherent strategies. Moving forward, the government could consider consolidating operational responsibility into a smaller number of ministries.

Technical assistance from development partners and from countries that have overcome similar policy challenges can play a role in building capacity at national and state/regional levels. Participants in the policy dialogue events highlighted this potential, and many of the proposals for action identified the need for technical assistance.

Combat corruption and perceptions of corrupt behaviour

Corruption at all levels, from high-level cronyism and nepotism to petty corruption, can undermine the process of building a national consensus. The government has stepped up its efforts to fight corruption during the recent reform period, and continued efforts will be needed to remove the opportunities for corruption and to challenge any culture of corruption moving forward. Measures that could help achieve this goal include setting out and publishing clear criteria for policy and administrative decisions. This should reduce the ability for decision makers to exercise undue discretion, thereby reducing the appearance of arbitrary decisions made without consideration on merits. Another measure would be to increase transparency, monitoring and evaluation in the planning process. Examples have been noted earlier, including increased transparency for receipts of revenue from the use of natural resources.

Managing migration and structural transformation

The migration of people within Myanmar (e.g. from rural to urban areas) and to other countries was seen by some participants as a potential obstacle to development, particularly the emigration of young people from rural areas and any resulting reduction in agricultural output. Official figures put the stock of Myanmar nationals living abroad at 514 000 (World Bank, 2011), but this does not take into account unofficial migration. Other estimates place the real number closer to 5.5 million (Mon, 2014), making Myanmar's emigration rate particularly high, even when compared with other "high emigration" countries such as the Philippines (Figure 2.4).

Rural to urban migration is to be expected as part of the structural transformation process, but development strategies and policies can influence the process. Structural transformation generally entails a reduction in on-farm employment: as agriculture becomes more productive, fewer people are needed on farms to produce the same or greater output. This labour is then freed up to work in more productive sectors. In many countries, this process of industrialisation has been accompanied by a parallel process of urbanisation as people migrate to cities in search of higher-wage work. However, a development strategy based on fostering agricultural value chains that create off-farm jobs in rural areas would provide alternative opportunities to those in urban areas, and could attenuate and complement the urbanisation process.

Although further research might be needed to more accurately gauge the impact of migration, the issue is intertwined with much of the discussion thus far. This includes a lack of land security, low incomes and the lack of a cost-effective formal financial system for remittances. Stakeholders saw more job opportunities, higher incomes and improved land laws as some of the key ways to limit the negative effects of migration, along with more formal arrangements for migration.

Figure 2.4. **Around 10% of Myanmar's population is estimated to live abroad**

Emigration rates (%)

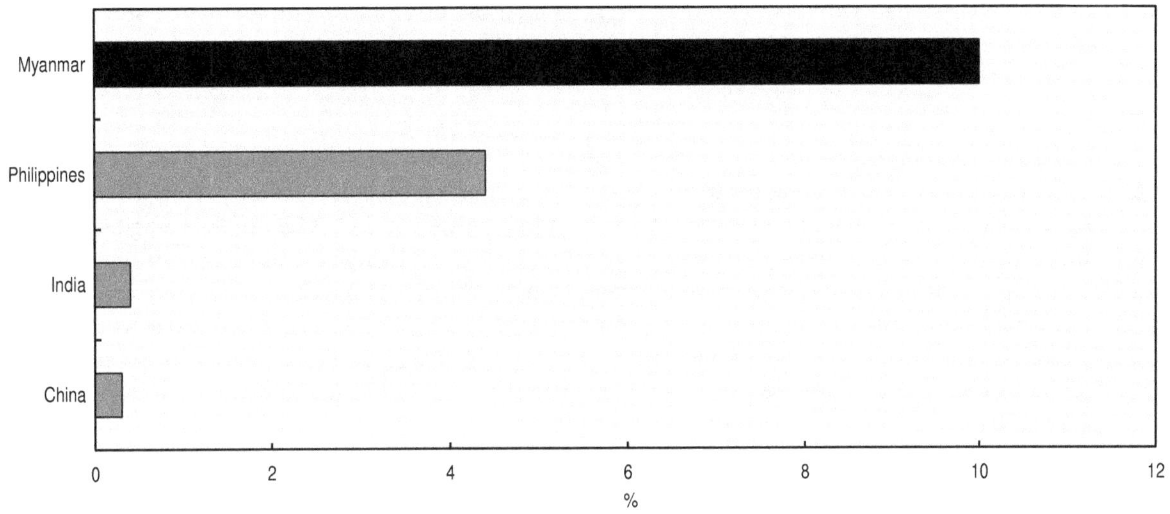

Myanmar
Philippines
India
China

0 2 4 6 8 10 12

%

Note: Myanmar data based on 2009 estimates; China, India and Philippines figures refer to 2005-06.

Sources: Mon (2014), "Mobility, identity and contributions of skilled Burmese migrant workers: An exploratory study in Bangkok 45", *ABAC Journal*, Vol. 34, No. 1; OECD (2012b), *Better Skills, Better Jobs, Better Lives: A Strategic Approach to Skills Policies, http://dx.doi.org/10.1787/9789264177338-en.*

StatLink http://dx.doi.org/10.1787/888933346870

Provide appropriate incentives for skilled workers to stay in Myanmar and for the diaspora to return

Myanmar will need policies to encourage its skilled workers to remain in the country and to contribute their skills to the economy. Policies could also be put in place to encourage Myanmar workers who are currently abroad to return to the country after having built up relevant skills (Box 2.8). Effective policies will be especially important from 2015 when the ASEAN Economic Community (AEC) comes into being, enabling the free flow of skilled labour throughout the ten ASEAN countries.

Experience has shown that the best way to reduce the emigration of workers is to provide incentives to stay, including by improving local labour-market conditions, rather than by imposing coercive measures to prevent emigration. Jobs in rural areas could be a focal point in this strategy given emigrant workers' expressed preference to return to their traditional homes. This strengthens the case for a development strategy based on an agricultural value chain approach that generates linkages with complementary services and inputs in the non-agricultural sector.

Formalising and capitalising on migration

Migration can be better managed through a formal system. The government could continue its efforts to provide migrants with formal documents, as well as work with neighbouring governments to legalise and register workers from Myanmar.

Box 2.8. **Attracting talent back**

Some countries have succeeded in attracting back talent by creating favourable conditions for returnees and offering incentives, as the examples from Malaysia and the Philippines show. Aside from policies to actively attract nationals to return, some countries have policies to help returnees re-integrate, such as the "one stop shop" service provided by Saint Kitts and Nevis. Permanent return can be a delicate issue, however, especially for high-skilled workers, who may experience difficulty finding employment opportunities matching their skills and interests. Countries can therefore also promote brain circulation by encouraging high-skilled workers to return for short-term visits and to teach or take part in co-operative projects.

Malaysia

The *Malaysian Returning Expert Program* provides incentives for high-skilled nationals to return to Malaysia. The incentives include a 15% income tax for five years, tax exemption on the import of personal belongings and up to two cars, and permanent residency status for a foreign spouse and children. To be eligible for the programme, individuals must have Malaysian citizenship, have been living and working continuously for the last three years, be under no obligation to their employer to return to Malaysia, and have no outstanding scholarship bonds or loans from the Malaysian government. The programme also takes into consideration other criteria designed to identify the highest skilled workers or those with particular work experience abroad in a national key economic area or sector. If accepted onto the programme, participants have two years to find a job and return to Malaysia in order to receive the benefits.

A recent assessment found that acceptance to the programme significantly increases the return probability of applicants with an existing job offer and female applicants without a Malaysian spouse (del Carpio et al, 2015). A fiscal cost-benefit analysis showed that it generates positive tax revenues and therefore effectively pays for itself.

Philippines

The *Assist WELL* programme in the Philippines provides returnees with specialised training in order to transition from the low-skilled work they have been performing abroad into occupations requiring higher qualifications. Specifically, the programme aims to re-train household service workers as teachers and find them employment in schools in their hometown. Returnees can also opt to work in non-teaching and other occupations in both government and private sectors in the Philippines.

Saint Kitts and Nevis

The government of Saint Kitts and Nevis established a Returning Nationals Secretariat, intended to be a "one stop shop" to provide information, guidance, and to help eliminate any delays associated with the relocation process. The assistance is available to any national of Saint Kitts and Nevis who has lived abroad for at least ten years who wants to return (along with their spouse and dependents) as well as Saint Kitts and Nevis nationals who have been deported from another country. The Secretariat offers assistance in finding jobs, housing, and accessing social services, and in some cases makes provisions for counselling.

Source: OECD/J. Gagnon/D. Khoudour-Castéras (2011), *Tackling the Policy Challenges of Migration: Regulation, Integration, Development*, Development Centre Studies, *http://dx.doi.org/10.1787/9789264126398-en*; Website of the Reintegration Center for OFWs, Department of Labor and Employment, Republic of Philippines, 2015 *http://nrco.dole.gov.ph/index.php/programs-and-services/sa-pinas-ikaw-ang-ma-am-sir*; Del Carpio, Ozden, Testaverde and Wagner (2015), "Reversing Brain Drain: Evidence from Malaysia's Returning Expert Program"; Saint Kitts and Nevis website: *www.stkittsnevisuk.com/index.php/returning-nationals?format=pdf*.

The potential benefits of migration could also be encouraged by lowering the cost of remittances. This could be done by increasing competition in the banking sector, which would in turn come from continued banking reforms as discussed in the previous section on finance.

Note

1. Subsistence-level farms are defined here as farms of less than two hectares. It should be noted that some farms of less than two hectares could generate income if high value crops – such as fruits, tea or herbs – are grown.

References

Blindenbacher, R. (2010), *The Black Box of Governmental Learning: The Learning Spiral– A Concept to Organize Learning in Governments*, World Bank, Washington, DC.

CSO (2013), *Myanmar Data: CD-ROM 2011-12*, Central Statistical Organization, Ministry of National Planning and Economic Development, Nay Pyi Taw, Myanmar.

Da Silva, C. (2009), "Commodity associations: A tool for supply chain development", Food and Agriculture Organization, Rome.

Del Carpio, Ozden, Testaverde and Wagner (2015), "Reversing Brain Drain: Evidence from Malaysia's Returning Expert Program".

Galvez-Nogales, E. (2010), *Agro-based Clusters in Developing Countries: Staying Competitive in a Globalised World*, Food and Agriculture Organization, Rome.

Guo, H., R. Jolly and J. Zhu (2005), "Contract farming in China: Supply chain or ball and chain?", presented at the *Annual World Symposium, IAMA*, Chicago, 25-26 June.

Hue, N.H. (2004), "Contract farming in Vietnam", *www.fao.org/fileadmin/user_upload/contract_farming/presentations/Contract_farming_in_Viet Nam.pdf.*

Jones, C. and M. Webber (2010), "Achieving synergies through clustering – Kenyan avocados", C.W Webber and P. Labaste (eds.), *Building Competitiveness in Africa's Agriculture: A Guide to Value Chains Concepts and Applications*, World Bank, Washington, DC.

Kloeppinger-Todd and Sandar (2013), "Rural finance in Myanmar", *Background Paper, No.* 3 prepared for the Strategic Agricultural Sector and Food Security Diagnostic for Myanmar, led by Michigan State University and in partnership with the Myanmar Development Resource Institute - Centre for Economic and Social Development (MDRI-CESD), January.

Kuczera, M., et al. (2008),*OECD Reviews of Vocational Education and Training: A Learning for Jobs Review of Sweden* 2008, OECD Reviews of Vocational Education and Training, OECD Publishing, Paris, *http://dx.doi.org/10.1787/9789264113978-en.*

Miyata, S., N. Minot and D. Hu (2009), "Impact of contract farming on income: Linking small farmers, packers and supermarkets in China", *World Development*, Vol. 37:11, pp. 1781-1790.

Mon, M. (2014), "Mobility, identity and contributions of skilled Burmese migrant workers: An exploratory study in Bangkok 45", *ABAC Journal*, Vol. 34, No. 1, Assumption University of Thailand, *www.abacjournal.au.edu/.*

MOAI (2013), *Report on Myanmar Census of Agriculture* 2010, Ministry of Agriculture and Irrigation, Nay Pyi Taw, Myanmar.

OECD, UMFCCI and UNESCAP (2014), *Myanmar Business Survey* (database).

OECD (2015a), *Multi-dimensional Review of Myanmar: Volume 2. In-depth Analysis and Recommendations*, OECD Development Pathways, OECD Publishing, Paris, *http://dx.doi.org/10.1787/9789264220577-en.*

OECD (2015b), *OECD Guidelines on Corporate Governance of State-Owned Enterprises, 2015 Edition*, OECD Publishing, Paris, *http://dx.doi.org/10.1787/9789264244160-en.*

OECD (2014a), *OECD Investment Policy Reviews: Myanmar 2014*, OECD Publishing, Paris, *http://dx.doi.org/10.1787/9789264206441-en.*

OECD (2014b), *Open Government Review of Myanmar.*

OECD (2013), *Multi-dimensional Review of Myanmar: Volume 1. Initial Assessment*, OECD Development Pathways, OECD Publishing, Paris, *http://dx.doi.org/10.1787/9789264202085-en.*

OECD (2012a), *Regulatory Consultation: A MENA-OECD Practitioners' Guide for engaging Stakeholders in the rule-making process.*

OECD (2012b), *Better Skills, Better Jobs, Better Lives: A Strategic Approach to Skills Policies*, OECD Publishing, Paris, *http://dx.doi.org/10.1787/9789264177338-en.*

OECD (2008), *OECD Review of Agricultural Policies: Chile 2008*, OECD Publishing, Paris, *http://dx.doi.org/10.1787/9789264042247-en*.

OECD/J. Gagnon/D. Khoudour-Castéras (2011), *Tackling the Policy Challenges of Migration: Regulation, Integration, Development*, Development Centre Studies, OECD Publishing, Paris, *http://dx.doi.org/10.1787/9789264126398-en*.

Prowse, M. (2012), *Contract Farming in Developing Countries – A Review*, Agence Française de Développement, Paris.

Rudolph, H. (2009), "State Financial Institutions: Mandates, Governance, and Beyond", *Policy Research Working Paper 5141*, World Bank, Washington, DC.

Ruth, K. and P. Grollman (2009), "Monitoring VET systems of major EU competitor countries", *ITB-Forschungsberichte, 39/2009*.

Seibel, H. D. and M. Ozaki (2009), "*Restructuring of state-owned financial institutions: Lessons from Bank Rakyat Indonesia*", Asian Development Bank, Mandaluyong City.

UNESCO (2014), *UNESCO Institute for Statistics Data Centre* (database), United Nations Educational, Scientific and Cultural Organization, *http://stats.uis.unesco.org/*.

United Nations (2013), *National Accounts Main Aggregates* (database), *http://unstats.un.org/unsd/snaama/resQuery.asp*.

Webber and P. Labaste (eds.), *Building Competitiveness in Africa's Agriculture: A Guide to Value Chains Concepts and Applications*, World Bank, Washington, DC.

World Bank (2014), *Global Food Chain Partnerships*, World Bank, Washington DC, *www.worldbank.org/en/topic/agriculture/brief/global-food-safety-partnership*.

World Bank (2011), *Migration and Remittances Factbook 2011*, World Bank, Washington, DC.

Conclusion

The *Multi-dimensional Review of Myanmar* began with a broad assessment of the country's development opportunities and constraints, and diagnosed structural transformation as the core development challenge. Agricultural modernisation and rural development more broadly were identified as a means to accelerate the process of structural transformation. Building linkages from agriculture to complementary non-agricultural activities – an "agricultural value chain" approach – could transition Myanmar from an agrarian economy to one based more on a mix of modern activities, including manufacturing and services. This would be an important strand of a broader development strategy for Myanmar that also includes strategies for developing the manufacturing and service sectors and making use of Myanmar's rich natural resource wealth.

Given Myanmar's level of economic development, its large rural population, the weight of agriculture in the economy and the number of people that are employed in agriculture, a development strategy that puts agriculture and rural development at its core has the potential to significantly improve the lives of millions of people.

As identified through the Review's multi-stakeholder policy dialogue events, the process of economic modernisation starting with the rural sector would require action in several areas:

- Supporting the agri-food sector's ability to respond to market demand for products that meet international safety and quality requirements.
- Introducing innovative models of delivering extension services and training to upgrade agronomic and technical skills.
- Providing the conditions for a vibrant financial system comprising a broad range of financial institutions and services that meet the needs of farmers, entrepreneurs and businesses in rural areas.
- Strengthening land rights by resolving any conflicts and ambiguity in the regulatory framework for land tenure and crop choice.
- Engaging citizens in the policy-making process through regular consultations and participatory approaches.
- Managing and maximising the benefits of the emigration of people from rural areas that often takes place as part of the structural transformation process.

This prioritisation exercise could serve as a useful first step in an iterative process of strategy building. Going forward, the successful implementation of any development strategy would be aided by detailed, costed action plans with clearly defined responsibilities, underpinned by a system for ongoing monitoring and evaluation.

Building capacity in Myanmar's institutions for policy making and implementation will also be essential. Designing the details and implementing such a development strategy would require expertise, coherence and co-ordination spanning several sectors and policy areas, as the list of actions above shows. Myanmar can benefit from the re-engagement of development partners with the country, and indeed many partners are already actively supporting public sector capacity building through their programmes.

Myanmar has embarked on a path of reform with an impressive pace that is likely to only increase as the country embeds its democracy. It will be crucial to sustain this drive in order to improve the conditions for development and ultimately people's well-being.

ORGANISATION FOR ECONOMIC CO-OPERATION AND DEVELOPMENT

The OECD is a unique forum where governments work together to address the economic, social and environmental challenges of globalisation. The OECD is also at the forefront of efforts to understand and to help governments respond to new developments and concerns, such as corporate governance, the information economy and the challenges of an ageing population. The Organisation provides a setting where governments can compare policy experiences, seek answers to common problems, identify good practice and work to co-ordinate domestic and international policies.

The OECD member countries are: Australia, Austria, Belgium, Canada, Chile, the Czech Republic, Denmark, Estonia, Finland, France, Germany, Greece, Hungary, Iceland, Ireland, Israel, Italy, Japan, Korea, Luxembourg, Mexico, the Netherlands, New Zealand, Norway, Poland, Portugal, the Slovak Republic, Slovenia, Spain, Sweden, Switzerland, Turkey, the United Kingdom and the United States. The European Union takes part in the work of the OECD.

OECD Publishing disseminates widely the results of the Organisation's statistics gathering and research on economic, social and environmental issues, as well as the conventions, guidelines and standards agreed by its members.

OECD DEVELOPMENT CENTRE

The Development Centre of the Organisation for Economic Co-operation and Development was established in 1962 and comprises 26 member countries of the OECD: Belgium, Chile, the Czech Republic, Denmark, Finland, France, Germany, Greece, Iceland, Ireland, Israel, Italy, Korea, Luxembourg, Mexico, the Netherlands, Norway, Poland, Portugal, Slovak Republic, Slovenia, Spain, Sweden, Switzerland, Turkey and the United Kingdom. In addition, 24 non-OECD countries are full members of the Development Centre: Brazil (since March 1994); India (February 2001); Romania (October 2004); Thailand (March 2005); South Africa (May 2006); Egypt and Viet Nam (March 2008); Colombia (July 2008); Indonesia (February 2009); Costa Rica, Mauritius, Morocco and Peru (March 2009); the Dominican Republic (November 2009); Senegal (February 2011); Argentina and Cabo Verde (March 2011); Panama (July 2013); Côte d'Ivoire, Kazakhstan and Tunisia (January 2015); the People's Republic of China (July 2015) and Ghana and Uruguay (October 2015). The European Union also takes part in the work of the Centre.

The Development Centre occupies a unique place within the OECD and in the international community. It provides a platform where developing and emerging economies interact on an equal footing with OECD members to promote knowledge sharing and peer learning on sustainable and inclusive development. The Centre combines multidisciplinary analysis with policy dialogue activities to help governments formulate innovative policy solutions to the global challenges of development. Hence, the Centre plays a key role in the OECD's engagement efforts with non-member countries.

To increase the impact and legitimacy of its work, the Centre adopts an inclusive approach and engages with a variety of governmental and non-governmental stakeholders. It works closely with experts and institutions from its member countries, has established partnerships with key international and regional organisations and hosts networks of private-sector enterprises, think tanks and foundations working for development. The results of its work are discussed in experts' meetings as well as in policy dialogues and high-level meetings, and are published in a range of high-quality publications and papers for the research and policy communities.

For more information on the Centre, please see *www.oecd.org/dev*.

OECD PUBLISHING, 2, rue André-Pascal, 75775 PARIS CEDEX 16
(41 2016 08 1P1) ISBN 978-92-64-25653-8 – 2016

www.ingramcontent.com/pod-product-compliance
Lightning Source LLC
LaVergne TN
LVHW081422110826
845149LV00010B/1837